WHO LEFT THE CORK OUT OF MY LUNCH?

Middle Age, Modern Marriage & Other Complications

VIKKI CLAFLIN

booktrope

Booktrope Editions
Seattle, WA 2016

Cover Design by Michelle Fairbanks
Edited by Kathryn Galan

PRINT ISBN 978-1-5137-0571-2
EPUB ISBN 978-1-5137-0622-1
Library of Congress Control Number: 2016900573

RAVE REVIEWS

Who Left the Cork Out of My Lunch?
Middle Age, Modern Marriage & Other Complications

"Reading Vikki's book is really about laughing at yourself, because in every line of her writing, you'll see you."
~ Diane Fitzpatrick, Author, *Great-Grandma is on Twitter and Other Signs the Rapture is Near*

"All the crazy nuances, frustrations, hilarious and heartfelt moments of our midlife years are brilliantly documented with humor and razor sharp candor."
~ Ellen Dolgen, *EllenDolgen.com*

"Not only will you find yourself laughing at her hilarious take on everyday life, but she shares her serious side with advice on love, marriage, and keeping it all together (including the places that jiggle)."
~ Cheryl Nicholl, *apleasanthouse.com*

"I read this book on public transportation, and because of my raucous laughing, the seat next to me remained vacant."
~ Haralee Weintraub, CEO, *Haralee.com Sleepwear*

"You'll laugh yourself into a good mood while you learn life's lessons."
~ Paul Brads, *rednecklatteravings.com*

"Whether touching the heart or unleashing her sharp wit, Vikki Claflin's stories are comedic perfection."
~ Linda Maltz Wolff, *carpoolgoddess.com*

"I laughed out loud and thought 'So it's not just me!' many times."
~ Tara Reed, *pivottohappy.com*

"Vikki is the kind of woman you want as your BFF, because she'll tell you like it is, all while serving you chocolate and copious amounts of wine!"
~ Rena McDaniel, *thediaryofanalzheimerscaregiver.com*

"Sure, you've become more 'Ma'am' than MILF,' but that doesn't mean there isn't plenty of great stuff still in store for you. What's there to laugh about at midlife? This book will let you know!"
~ Ronna Benjamin, *betterafter50.com*

"What makes comedy truly funny is the authenticity aspect of it. This compilation of chapters will resonate with females around the world!"
~ Jodie Filogomo, *jtouchofstyle.com*

"Vikki writes with the perfect balance of humor and heart. You'll laugh out loud. You'll have those 'aha' moments. And even better, you'll learn to love the person you've become. Just as Vikki has."
~ Janie Emaus, *janieemaus.com*

"I loved *Who Left the Cork Out of My Lunch?* the way I love eating anything that has the words "salted caramel" in it, or not going to work."
~ Michelle Combs, *rubbershoesinhell.com*

"No one writes humor better. Her rollicking, sometimes irreverent account of life in her equally hilarious family is a great read and a great gift for a mother, sister or BFF."
~ Carol Cassara, *carolcassara.com*

"Hysterical doesn't quite do this book justice. Love, love, love!"
~ Kathy Radigan, *mydishwasherspossessed.com*

"I didn't simply enjoy this, I laughed out loud through the entire book."
~ Doreen McGettigan, *doreenmcgettigan.com*

"I'm proud to be part of Vikki Claflin's 'Big Girl Panties Society,' and reading her book reminds me of how great it is to be a midlife warrior!"
~ Sharon Greenthal, *emptyhousefullmind.com*

ACKNOWLEDGMENTS

To my fabulous team from Booktrope. Pam Labbe, Kathryn Galán, Michelle Fairbanks, and Samantha Zeiner. Thank you for bringing my manuscript to life. Your talents, enthusiasm, and unwavering support made this adventure so much fun. I will be forever grateful.

To Hubs. My inspiration, my rock, and my most enthusiastic fan. Thank you for letting me splatter our private life all over the Internet and for still being there every morning when I wake up.

Table of Contents

CHAPTER 1
The Big Girl Panties Society: Rules for Membership

"I've yet to hear a man ask for advice on how to combine marriage and a career."
—Gloria Steinham

THE FIRST TIME I HEARD someone say, "Put on your big girl panties and deal with it," I burst out laughing and spit my wine across my computer keyboard. My mind had an instant visual of a middle-aged woman sword fighting in nothing but her underwear. My brain goes places others' don't.

I decided then and there to start up a "Big Girl Panties Society," created to celebrate midlife women warriors.

We've been through our twenties, when anything was possible. We wanted it all, and we wanted it all at the same time. And we believed we could have it.

Through our thirties, we were focused on career climbing, finding potential soul mates, raising future world leaders, and struggling to make mortgage payments for houses we couldn't afford.

By forty, we began to come to terms with who we were and what drove us or made us happy. And we began weeding out what didn't. Many of us were on our second marriages and bearing the battle scars of divorce.

Now we're fifty-something and a bit like the Velveteen Rabbit. He's a little worn, with an ear lopped off, a button or two missing, and seams no longer straight, but a better bunny for his journey. We're independent, irreverent, opinionated, and fiercely loyal to those we love. We diet if we choose to, but cheat with no apologies. Exercise activities are selected as much for their fun factor as for their ability to give us firm thighs. We've discovered that spoiling our grandchildren is easier than raising our kids. We've traded stupid stilettos for fabulous flats, and we're still hot. Sex is better than ever because we've learned what we want and we ask for it. We're happiest when we're surrounded by friends, sharing a great bottle of wine and laughing 'til our faces hurt.

If you're a woman warrior, you're in. But like any club, there are a few rules for membership:

1. You should have experienced some level of menopause. This gives you street cred when the group conversation inevitably turns to how to deal with night sweats and fatigue. We lose patience with thirty-year-old Beach Barbies claiming they'll never take drugs for menopause symptoms because it's a *natural* process. It makes us want to smack you and make notes to remind your future estrogen-popping self what a bad-ass you were at thirty.

2. You should have a rudimentary knowledge of music from the '70s and '80s. At least enough to know that Kanye didn't "discover" Paul McCartney. How else will you be able to join our nostalgic, wine-induced, group karaoke during girls' night out?

3. We request that all cell phones be turned off or put on vibrate during group meetings. This includes luncheons, spa days, wine tastings, book club gatherings, in-home retail parties, and shopping excursions. This is *our* time.

4. You must not use the word "like" more than once in any single sentence.

5. No comments or quips shall be made about the group's 10 p.m. curfew. If you want to stay and boogie-oogie-oogie (and you should know what that means) until last call, slip quietly into the women's bathroom until we've all gone home.

6. You must be a grandma, be pushing your offspring to make you a grandma, or at least have a grandma in your immediate peer group. This helps us establish that you share the same historical time frame as the rest of the group. And if your boobs haven't yet fallen off their perch and migrated to your waistline, you have an unfair advantage when it comes time for our coveted annual summer "Best Boob-Belt" award.

7. You cannot be offended by swearing. We've earned it.

8. At any group gathering that involves food, there will be no mention of weight, calories, or diets. We're sixty. We get to eat.

9. There must be at least one current fashion trend in your closet that you're wearing the second time around.

10. You should be able to recognize at least two elevator songs as being ones you dated to in your twenties. Extra points are given if you have the original songs on your iPod.

11. You must be willing to view dozens of photos of grandchildren, while listening to lengthy, detailed examples that prove unequivocally that the tiny tot is obviously gifted. (He can already count to 3!) Requests within the group for references on little Henry's pre-application into Johns Hopkins, Class of 2032, must be honored.

12. You must agree to share names and contact information, if asked, about where you got that gorgeous handbag, who cuts your hair, or who does your Botox.

13. No whining. The purpose of our group is to provide support and encouragement to each other. While we're always willing to lend a shoulder and some advice (if you ask), your repeated, prolonged wailing about circumstances you have no intentions of changing will be respectfully removed from the agenda.

14. What is said among the group, stays in the group. We're not in high school. Tattling or rumor-spreading about any other member will get your ass summarily booted out the door.

15. You must be able to laugh at yourself. Various body parts have shifted downward like underground fault lines. Hair has stopped growing on our heads, but is now sprouting on our chins. Thighs jiggle when we're standing still. We gain weight on two Cheerios and a Diet Coke. We wear "age-appropriate" clothing. We have to record any show we want to watch that comes on after 10 p.m. We love sex, but we're usually too tired to have it. If you don't see anything funny about this, we're probably not the group for you.

I suspect that there are lots of women warriors out there. Let's find each other and celebrate. We're *fabulous*.

CHAPTER 2

Good Morning, Mom.
Now, for the Love of God, Put Some Clothes On

"I get whatever placidity I have from my father. But my mother taught me how to take it on the chin."
—Norma Shearer

MY SON WAS DEPLOYED for a year to Iraq with the National Guard, and anticipating my daily maternal meltdowns at *how far away* he would for the next year (sob!), he set me up on Skype before he left, so we could video chat with each other from time to time.

Notwithstanding that it's *not* like NCIS on TV, where the video and audio are crystal clear and totally synced as if the person is standing in the room with you (It's a little grainy, with a definite time delay on the speech), I did get to see his beautiful smile and hear those magic words, "Hi, Mom," every few weeks.

Whenever Jake's Skype call came in, my computer would emit a tinkling sound, like a tiny bell. Since there's a significant time difference between Oregon and Iraq, this often happened in the middle of the night. If I missed the call, it might be days or weeks before another one came, so I developed ears like a mama fruit bat for that sound. I could hear it from any room of the house, any time of the day.

One hot, sticky summer night, I was lying in bed when I heard the much-anticipated bell sound from down the hall. I bolted out of bed and raced down the hall to click the bright green "Answer Call" icon on my screen before he hung up or we got cut off due to unreliable phone connections. Jake's smiling face popped up, and I felt a surge of maternal relief to see he was okay, until I heard, "*OH*

MY GOD, Mom! Are you *NAKED*?" I looked down and realized, to my horror, I was wearing Hubs's boxers and *nothing else.*

I immediately dove to the floor, taking out the chair on my way down, and crawled on two knees and one hand over to Hubs's closet for a T-shirt, while frantically waving my other arm up in front of the computer, yelling, "Wait! Wait! Don't hang up!!" I could hear raucous laughter from the background, as Jake's Army buddies figured out what was going on.

Jake was shouting "Mom! *MOM!* Click the 'audio only' button! It's on your left! Audio Only!"

"No, wait!" I cried, "I'm here! *Don't hang up!"* I kept yelling until I'd finally grabbed an oversize shirt to pull over my head, and scrambled up off the floor to get back in front of the computer, suitably attired to video chat with my offspring.

Jake looked at me and said, dryly, "You realize that when I get back home and anyone asks me what the most traumatic thing I saw over here was, I'm going to have to say *'My Mother.'"*

Apparently you're never too old to scar your kids for life.

CHAPTER 3
Doctor, Can You Give Me a Lift?

"A male gynecologist is like an auto mechanic who never owned a car."
—Carrie Snow

WHEN I WAS IN MY LATE FORTIES, I decided to get my breasts lifted. I didn't want them *bigger*. Just *higher*. Back up where the good Lord put them before gravity and age began to coax them closer to my naval than my clavicles. There's just something about looking in the mirror every morning at two sad beagle ears attached to your upper torso that screams *National Geographic, the Pictorial Edition*. Not to mention that most of my friends had had implants or lifts ten years earlier, so even women older than me had younger-looking bodies because they were, well, *perky*, and I looked more like a '60s love child who hadn't worn a bra since puberty.

So, armed with photos of young starlets and their up-to-*there* breasts, I made an appointment with a well-recognized plastic surgeon to discuss my options. I entered his plush office, with its thick, toe-sinking carpet and quietly cascading waterfall in the corner; his impossibly-perfect receptionist guided me back to the softly-lit (for which I would thank God in the next half hour) exam room, and she flashed me a bright smile as she instructed me to remove my shirt and bra and wait for the doctor.

Twenty minutes later, Doc walked in (Is it me, or do they *all* look twelve years old?), introduced himself, and, obviously not into foreplay, reached over and lifted one breast, checking for "bounce." (Say hello to the point, you arrogant puppy. If they still *bounced*, I wouldn't *be* there.). Then he let it go; it promptly slammed back down onto my chest like a wrecking ball taking out a high rise.

Next he stuck a piece of blue litmus-type paper underneath one, waited several seconds, and pulled the paper out to check for skin-on-skin contact, which would show up as "light moisture." The paper looked like a Bounty Quicker-Picker-Upper. By then, my self-esteem had fled the building (presumably looking for the closest bar, which was where I was headed as soon as I could find my bra).

Then he stuck a large piece of white paper underneath both breasts and *traced them*. The final picture looked like two carrots lying on a table. I was so mortified by that time, I hardly noticed the *up close and personal Polaroids* that he took. One for each carrot.

Oh. My. God.

When he *finally* finished his exam, I stammered out that I'd read about a procedure where they could go in from the armpit and pull the ligaments up, which was less invasive and left fewer scars. Without missing a beat, he replied, "That would've worked if you had come in ten years ago. You're *way* past that now." At which point he calmly left the room, leaving me with instructions to make an appointment on my way out. *Yeah, no.* I scrambled into my clothes and headed home like an old plow horse to the barn.

When I explained why I was so upset, Hubs asked, "Why do you even want to do this? Why don't you just wear one of those shove-em-up bras?" I explained that that only worked until I took the bra *off*; then everybody would know what they really looked like.

"Who the hell is *everybody*?" he choked out. "How many people are you thinking will be in the room whenever you take your bra off?" Well, after *today*, I would say *nobody. Ever.*

I ultimately decided the lift was not for me. My boobs and I would grow old together, and when I die, Hubs knows to bury me in my best sports bra. $85 a pop and virtually guaranteed to hold the sisters in place long enough for friends to sigh, "And she was so *young*."

CHAPTER 4
Menopause Killed My Inner MILF

"I had my first hot flash yesterday and was told by a good friend that Merlot and chocolate help. Menopause may not be so bad after all."
—Anjie Henley

GOOGLE "BENEFITS OF MENOPAUSE," and you'll get 8,570,000 possible links. Over *eight and a half million articles* written on how menopause makes us stronger, sexier, more confident, and more at peace with our bodies and our sexuality. Not to mention the exhilarating freedom from periods, bloating, cramping, PMS, and the constant worry about pregnancy, however slim the chance.

What they don't tell you in those same posts is that all that Zen is achieved only after menopause is completely *over*. It's the prize at the end of a rather bumpy ride, during which you'll start questioning whether you'll ever be sexy again. Or if you'll ever care.

Like most women, I like feeling attractive, sexy, and *desirable*. I've spent more money than I probably should've towards that goal over the years, and although yoga pants and no makeup are my norm, I do clean up fairly well (which admittedly takes longer with each passing year). I have a tiny, but persistent, inner hot chick who still likes stilettos, little black dresses, and the appreciative looks from Hubs at my efforts. Menopause crashed my hotness with a thud heard in three states.

Suddenly I was more "Ma'am" than MILF. Men stopped whistling at me from the street and started helping me through the crosswalk. People no longer commented, "You look so much like your mother" and started assuming we were sisters.

In retrospect, I'm amazed that Hubs made it through my menopausal years. He married a reasonably confident, arguably-normal woman, and woke up one day to an overheated, moody, questionably-sane female sobbing uncontrollably over the sudden appearance of cankles. My MILF was gone. How menopause killed it:

1. Hot flashes. We were out at our favorite romantic restaurant, and, instead of the coy flirting of our early years ("Gee, Big Guy, is it hot in here or is it just you?"), it became, "Is it hot in here or what? I'm *hot*. Is *anybody else hot*?" Repeated requests to the apparently deaf waiter to turn the thermostat down finally ended with a screeching, "Can't you turn the *freaking heat down*? It's *Too Friggin' Hot in Here!*" Hubs dragged my sweaty body out of the restaurant, and we haven't been back since.

2. Metabolism changes. Actually, mine didn't change. It stopped. Weight maintenance was now limited to one Fruit Loop and a Diet Coke per day. Weight *loss* required colonic cleansing and fasting. And, if you like wine, no carbs for you. Ever. Carbs plus wine make you blow up like a puffer fish, so you have to choose. I haven't had a carb since 2009.

3. Fatigue. I was tired *all the time*. Bedtime went from 10:30 p.m. to 8:30 p.m., effectively eliminating boogie nights on the dance floor, since it's virtually impossible to find a band that starts at 5:30.

4. Night sweats. Yeah, nothing turns a man on more than being whacked on the arm at 2 a.m. to "Get up" because we have to change the cold, wet sheets. Again. After the first six months, we both got used to just tossing beach towels over the sheets and crawling back into bed. Take *that*, sex life.

5. Day sweats. I quit going to the gym after realizing my clothes would be soaked, with visible sweat pouring down between my boobs and my butt crack, after only being on the treadmill for three minutes. It took me longer to wipe down the machine than it did to work out.

6. Incontinence. I'd laugh. A little squirt. I'd sneeze. Another little squirt. The actual need to pee? Now I'd be clenching my Kegels while I waddle-ran to the nearest bathroom, praying there wasn't a line. By the end of the evening, I smelled like Eau de Pee, sitting in wet undies and wondering what the hell had happened to my life. Hubs, not surprisingly, was still not turned on.

7. Mood swings. Some days, Hubs would come home to find me sobbing over yet another Hallmark commercial about the son returning home at Christmas to his adoring little sister and happy, teary-eyed parents. Other days, any and all comments directed at me from anyone in the room on any subject were met with, "What the hell is *wrong* with you?" often accompanied by a smack up 'long side the head. Hubs claimed later that every day was a crap shoot.

8. Body changes. Under-arm twaddle, boobs headed towards my knees, and hips widening irrevocably eliminated anything sleeveless or low-cut from my closet and would forevermore require military-grade underwear. Menopause underwear is designed to git 'er *done*, by pushing, lifting, and shoving defiant and migrating body parts back into their original shape and place. We no longer care about lace edging or cute bows. We need Kevlar underwire and the Spanx Company on speed-dial.

9. Body heat. More consistent than hot flashes, I was basically just hot. All. The. Time. We had the front door open year-round, and unless it was raining, I had the top down on my car. In December. I turned the house heat completely off every night and opened all the windows. Hubs repeatedly complained that he couldn't perform in a meat locker. I reminded him once that it's a bad chef who blames his utensils, but apparently he didn't get my humor. Nobody got any *that* night.

10. Hunger. Suffice it to say that I was *always* hungry. And somehow, I have no recollection of craving carrots. I *do* remember threatening to bludgeon Hubs to death one night for eating the last of my Milk Duds. To this day, he's never eaten another Dud.

11. Evening conversations tended more towards chronic menopause-induced IBS than our mutual plans for our next vacation through the wine country. Hubs, who's never seen me pee (*not once* in fifteen years) because I want to maintain a modicum of mystery in our marriage, looked a bit stunned one night when I bent over and hiked up the back of my dress, asking "When I bend over like this, can you see cellulite on the backs of my legs?" He laughed so hard, he fell off his chair, but was smart enough to leave that question untouched.

Now at the end of the tunnel, I'm approaching inner peace. But it was a humbling and often mortifying ride. And occasionally, when I'm doing my morning prayers and meditation, my thoughts will free-fall back to those years, and I'll ask God, "Really? *REALLY*?"

I'm still waiting for a response.

CHAPTER 5

How to Compliment Your Wife

"I have been complimented many times and they always embarrass me. I always feel they have not said enough."
—Mark Twain

IN AN EARLIER CONVERSATION with Hubs:

Me: "Does this bra make my boobs look perkier?"

Hubs: "Perkier than what?"

Me: "Perkier than before."

Hubs: "Before what?"

Me: "This isn't a trick question."

Hubs: "Okay. Maybe. I don't know. I don't think you should worry about it. We're all getting older, you know, and I think you look great no matter what your boobs look like."

Me: "What a horrible, mean thing to say!"

Hubs: "I was trying to give you a compliment!"

Me: "Well, you suck at it."

Hubs: "For the love of God, woman, next time give me cue cards."

I can do that.

Dashing down to my computer, I quickly typed up *Hubs's Guide for Complimenting His Wife*.

Assuming we've moved past the construction site approach, including the juvenile ("Nice rack, baby") or the cheesy ("You have eyes a man could drown in"), neither of which is particularly effective on girls over twenty-two or who don't work at Hooters, let's begin with the basics.

1. Compliments should make us feel wanted, appreciated, and absolutely gorgeous. Every now and then, we want to feel like you still see us the way you did when we were first in love. Before the kids, our jobs, the mortgage payments, the dogs, the bills, the laundry, birthdays, and gravity all piled up and, we swapped our thongs and stilettos for yoga pants and T-shirts.

2. Be brief. Don't ramble. A girlfriend once told me that the best compliment she ever received from her husband was a single word. She came out of the bedroom, dressed for date night and a bit self-conscious in her rarely-worn, strappy little black dress. He stopped, looked at her for a moment, and said, "Wow." (That night was the best sex they'd had for months. Personally, I don't believe in coincidences.)

3. Be specific. "You're pretty" is great, but "That dress makes your legs look a mile long" will be happily repeated to her BFF tomorrow morning over coffee, and you'll look like a rock star.

4. Pay Attention. Assuming she at least occasionally does something that surprises or impresses you (if not, that's another discussion entirely), mention it. "You're so patient with your little niece. You handled it beautifully when she set your office on fire" or "You were great with my parents today. And thank you for not decking Uncle Buck when he pinched your ass at our wedding… twice" will go a long way towards making her feel special.

5. Surprise her. A spontaneous "I'm glad I married you" while you're watching TV will put an instant smile on her face. In other words, don't save it for when you want to get laid or you're trying to end an argument.

6. Try to make the compliment about her. "Great boots" is nice, but "You look hot in those boots" is *much* better.

7. Tell the truth. Unless you've been living in a shack in the Ozark Mountains your entire life, with no cable or Internet service, "You're the most beautiful woman I've ever seen" is going to sound phony to any woman but Angelina Jolie. She knows that's not true, and now you have a credibility issue. It's like parents who tell their child he's the smartest person in the world. Sooner or later, little Billy is going to find out Mommy and Daddy were *lying* and now he doesn't believe a word they say. Pick something that's actually true about her. "You have a beautiful smile" (when, in fact, she does) is a better choice.

8. Avoid backhanded compliments. These are not compliments. They're insults that start out slowly. "You can speak French? Wow! I never would have guessed." Bite me, jackass. "A woman *should* be curvy. You look healthy." I guarantee you we just heard, "You're fat, but I'm not stupid enough to say that." Hope you like sleeping on the couch. "Love your new haircut, babe. Your face doesn't look as round." By now she's thinking, "OMG. So all this time, I've been walking around with a pumpkin head, and *only now* you're telling me?" This is where "Shoot the messenger" came to be. These are passive-aggressive shots and should be limited to no more than... well, none, if you want to stay married to this woman.

9. When in doubt, tell her she looks thinner than usual. Surveys report that 43% of women say that this is their favorite compliment *ever*. "You look so thin" will have us singing your praises all over town.

10. Things I Should Say to My Wife More Often. A few other tried and trues that men should always have in their Rolodex include: "You look gorgeous." "I love your body." "You're the most beautiful woman here tonight." "I'm proud to be seen with you." "I like the way you think." There are others, but consider this your starter set, which should keep you going for the next few weeks.

And now, in a recent conversation with Hubs:

Me: "I'm using a new cream. How does my skin look?"

Hubs: "Fine."

Me: "Fine??"

Hubs: "Oh, actually, you look stunning, and I wish I could stay home and stare at you all day, repeatedly reminding myself what a lucky, *lucky* man I am."

Me (with a bright smile, deliberately choosing to ignore the almost-imperceptible eye roll and snort-laugh that accompanied that statement): "Thank you, sweetie. I love you, too!"

Now, was that *so* hard??

CHAPTER 6

Food Diary, My Butt. That's a Paper Trail.

"Probably nothing in the world arouses more false hopes than the first four hours of a diet."
—Dan Bennett

RESEARCHING MY WEIGHT loss program options for 2016, in yet another enthusiastic but short-lived attempt to lose the same ten pounds I've been working on since 1974, I did a quick review of previous epic fails.

1. Jenny Craig®. Tastes great but portioned for a small gerbil. Jenny's Fish & Chips dinner entree would be more aptly named "Fish & *chip*." Hubs tried to take a bite of my breakfast sausage once, and I burst into tears. This plan is not for couples who like to share.

2. Nutrisystem®. Worst. Food. Ever. I should have clued in on the foil-wrapped entrees. Very space shuttle, with taste to match. Sorry, Ms. Osmond, but I couldn't get hungry enough to eat this food.

3. HCG Drops. Supposed to make your body think it's pregnant (Who *thinks* of this stuff?) Since I gained sixty-five pounds during my only pregnancy, this gets perilously close to what my son calls "Mom's dark place." Then I saw the 500 calories/day plan associated with the drops. 500 calories per day? What do you do after *breakfast*? Sigh. Back on the shelf for you.

4. Low Carb. This one works if you can live without bread. And rice. And wheat, potatoes, pasta, most fruits, ice cream, desserts, fried foods, or alcohol. Yep, that's right. *No red wine.* Positively uncivilized. And three days into it, I would have cheerfully traded my beloved Paco for a bagel. Buh-bye, Dr. Atkins.

5. Weight Watchers. Undeniably successful, if you enjoy spending your days searching recipes, grocery shopping, planning, cooking, counting, and charting your progress. Not for the uncommitted. Or for those with a job.

This was getting discouraging, until I discovered an online article that reported higher weight loss by people who wrote down everything they ate during the day. Well, that didn't sound too hard. Even *I* can do that. Happily printed off the form and started my food diary the next morning.

Breakfast: two slices bacon, two eggs, large cinnamon roll. Lunch: Nachos, extra guacamole. Afternoon snack: Peanut M&M's. (Hard to actually count, since they were in a bowl, but I *did* skip the nasty blue ones.) Dinner: Homemade lasagna, garlic bread. (No space provided for wine, so assuming they weren't asking for that.) Bedtime snack: Bowl of Lucky Charms with milk (skim… not like I'm not *trying*).

Two days later…Well, this is stupid. All I got was hand cramps from writing, and I didn't lose an ounce. I think I just have a slow metabolism.

CHAPTER 7
Thou Shall Not Tell a Lie. Unless Thou is Married

"I've learned that only two things are necessary to keep one's wife happy. First, let her think she's having her own way. And second, let her have it."
—Lyndon B. Johnson

WITH SOCIAL MEDIA BLOWING UP with posts about Valentine's Day and everyone anticipating the fat little cupid and the romantic gifts he'll leave behind, I got curious about some lesser-known holidays that we don't celebrate with quite the same national enthusiasm. A quick Google search came up with Laughing Day, Pork Rind Appreciation Day, International Sex Bomb Day, 50 Llamas Day, and OMG, *Honesty Day*.

I'm always entertained by couples who brag that they're "totally honest" with each other. These marital puppies have usually been legally wed for less than a year and have yet to learn that total honesty is to a marriage what a souped-up Mustang is to a new teenage driver… a crash just *waiting* to happen.

For the record, I'm not recommending you lie about life-altering issues. "Of course I want lots of children," when the truth is you can't stand any humans under the age of twenty, or "No, I most emphatically did *not* sleep with your best friend that weekend you went into rehab," when, in fact, you did, making you a complete douche who will eventually get caught by your wife or by karma. These are what researchers call "hard lies," noted for being self-serving and existing primarily to protect the liar.

"White lies" are told to protect the *other* person. When there's nothing to be gained by telling the "totally honest truth," a little white lie is often kinder. Bad haircuts, winter weight gain, a less-than-flattering but beloved pair of jeans: these are all fleeting. But she'll remember your "honest criticism" *forever*.

White lies can usually be defined by the alternate title, "Tell Me What I Want to Hear."

1. "I painted my office fuchsia. Isn't it *fabulous***?"** Your first thought was that all it's missing is a giant disco ball, but it's *her* office, and it's just paint. If she loves it, you love it.

2. "I have a headache. Otherwise, I'd be *so* **into sex with you right now."** This is the insurmountable, Great-Barrier-Reef excuse (impossible to dispute; you'll just have to take our word for it) for not feeling the duo-monkey dance at that moment. You can challenge the excuse ("You had a headache *last* week") and possibly overcome her sex-resistant ensemble of fleece sweats and your old T-shirt, but don't bother to ask, "Was it good for you?" She may be more honest than you'd like.

3. "Of *course* **I love your friends.** Who wouldn't love Tommy, who's *so* proud that he can drink the entire contents of our beer fridge every time he stops by? Or Jack, who never goes anywhere without his ninety-pound Pit Bull aptly named Diablo. They're just *hoots*." Tell Tommy to bring his own damn beer and ask Jack to leave Diablo at home, and she might stop slamming cupboard doors in the kitchen whenever the boys come over.

4. "Thanks, honey, I just *love* **it,"** when referring to your gift of arguably the ugliest sweater anyone ever paid money for. Over the past three decades in retail, I've heard dozens of women tell stories about gifts from Hubs that make them question if he's ever actually noticed what she wears, like, *ever*. "After fifteen years of marriage, he thinks I'm jonesing for a pink Hello Kitty sweater with a rhinestone message across my boobs that says 'I'm a Kitty Kat.' *Have we met*?" We either quietly return them or tuck them away somewhere. And if you ask, we'll say, "It's at the dry cleaners," because we hate the sweater, but we love you.

5. "Absolutely not," when, upon seeing a commercial for Botox, you ask if we'd ever do something that silly. The fact is we've been shelling out serious bucks over the past five years to slow the evidence of the passage of time, but it just never seemed the right time to toss out, "By the way, Honey Buns, I get botulism injected into my face four times a year. And how was *your* day?"

6. The uber-classic "Do these jeans make my butt look big?" which can *only* be answered with, "That's not possible."

7. "Do you really want to go to my family reunion in Omaha?" Not just "no." It's more of a "Oh *hell* no." But you can rock the answer with, "I'll go anywhere, as long as it's with you," significantly reducing episodes of sudden-onset migraines at bedtime (see #2).

8. "Do you think my sister is pretty?" Make no mistake. That question means *"prettier than me?"* A time-honored response is, "She's okay, but you definitely got the looks in your family." But "I've never noticed" is the MacDaddy you-*got*-this answer, especially if you can manage to look slightly confused at the question.

9. "My parents are fighting. Do you mind if my mother stays with us for a while?" Concede defeat at any question concerning her mother. By the time she asks this question, Mom is in the driveway. With a toothbrush.

10. "I told my sister we'd watch her two dogs this weekend so she and Hubs can get away. Is that okay?" Sissy's two dogs include a thousand-pound Great Dane and a Bull Mastiff currently undergoing pet therapy for anger issues, but she already said yes, so you can either look like a jerk who doesn't care about her sister's happiness, or you can throw a blanket into the garage and look like a hero. But no matter how you respond, the dogs are staying.

Hubs and I recently heard the Marital Lie in its purest form, in the dumbest movie *ever*, where the dying wife, gasping her last tragic breath, tells her husband she wants him to fall in love again and be happy without her. *I don't think so.* I told Hubs that that woman is stupid and it was just a *movie*.

If I go first, he's allowed a brief mourning period (two weeks ought to do it), then he's to keel over dead from a broken heart and join me in the afterlife so we can be together forever, *like he promised*.

In the meantime, go warm up the car. We're going to Great-Aunt Bertha's for dinner. Yes, she still has fifteen cats and a goiter. But you always said you liked her.

CHAPTER 8
Makeup Mistakes That Make You Look Older

"The most beautiful makeup for a woman is passion. But cosmetics are easier to buy."
—Yves Saint Laurent

I STARTED TEACHING MAKEUP application in the early '80s. I was living in Canada at the time, working as a training manager for Estee Lauder. For those of you who prefer visuals to statistics, we established the first Clinique counter in Western Canada. (Yes, I'm *that* old.)

Thirty-plus years later, having applied makeup on hundreds women of all ages, a few truisms have become apparent. One of the most important lessons in makeup application is that *age is a factor*. Simply put, you cannot wear the same makeup, in the same way, for your entire life.

We all get into beauty ruts. Routines that have served us well for years, that we're comfortable with. When you do the same thing over and over for years on end, you naturally get it down to speed-dial status. If you're cleaning your bathroom, this is good. But makeup suitable for a college student will make even the most beautiful mid-lifer look ten years older.

A perfect time for a makeup overhaul is around age fifty. After that fabulous birthday bash is over, after the bleary-eyed guests have all gone home and the *what-was-I-thinking* hangover is blessedly behind us, it's time to look in the mirror and accept that we are no longer able to pull off this year's trendy blue eyeshadow or our favorite deep-red lipstick that we've worn since we were thirty.

Department stores are a great place to test new products and colors, but women are often put off by the aggressive upselling from heavily made-up, commissioned, teenage salesgirls. And it can be awkward having your makeup redone by Goth Girl in the middle of the cosmetics department during lunch hour traffic.

So, after three decades in the industry, I thought I'd share a few tips for anyone who might be confused about what works and what doesn't after fifty. We'll start with what *doesn't*. And you don't even have to get dressed up or leave your house. Slip on your bunny slippers and your comfiest pj's, and grab a latte. Here you go.

1. **Heavy foundation.** Foundation should never be used as spackle. Its purpose is simply to smooth the skin tone, not fill in crevices or conceal menopausal acne. If you can't find one that goes on like a second skin, you need a new skin-care routine, not a new foundation.

2. **Foundation is the wrong color.** I see this one *a lot*. Women who want to look more tanned get a darker color that doesn't match the rest of their body, so their face always looks dirty. Too orange and you look like an oompa-loompa. Too much pink looks chalky. This is where you'll want to spend a little money and get professional advice. Unfortunately, you won't find this in stores that end in the word "Mart."

3. **Skipping the blusher.** As we age (don't we hate that expression?), the "bloom of youth" wears off, and we look washed out, less vibrant. Pale skin, lacking any visible blush of color, can make you look cadaver-ish, lacking a healthy pulse or discernible blood flow.

4. **Too much concealer.** Packing on the concealing stick underneath your eyes, trying to hide puffiness or dark circles, draws attention to this area by settling into expression lines around your eyes like bathtub caulking.

5. **Dark lipstick.** In your twenties and thirties, dark lipstick can look chic and sophisticated. After fifty, it tends to look bitchy. It also picks up yellow in your teeth, so unless they're piano-keys white, don't even think about it.

6. **Eyeliner around the entire eye.** This look is hard to pull off after thirty. It's too Biker Chick (and men hate it, btw). By fifty, if you have expression lines or eyelid sagging, this will make you look like Jax's mother on *Sons of Anarchy*. Leave the "smoky eyes" to your daughter.

7. **Too much bronzer.** Simply put, your face should not look like it just spent two weeks in Hawaii without the rest of you.

8. Obvious lip liner. This is the visible panty line (VPL) of the face. Fading lip lines can make the lips look thinner, less "lush" (hence the unfortunate Hollywood stampede for lip injections). Lip pencils are meant to gently define and fill out the lip lines, not outline them in a way that suggests people might not otherwise know where your mouth is.

9. Nude or no lip color. This is a big one. We lose pigment in our lips as we age, making us look pale or tired (read: *older*). Whether it's a peachy-pink Chanel lipstick or a sheer raspberry ChapStick, some color to our lips says that our blood is pumping and we're ready to leap tall buildings. That's a lot of bang from a tiny little tube of colored wax.

10. Too much powder. Women who routinely "powdered their nose" during the day in their younger years often still do that when they're in their fifties. It's time to *stop doing that*. Repeated applications of powder on skin that is thinner and drier can result in a dehydrated-looking, talc-layered face, with powder settled in every line and wrinkle. Remember Great-Grandma Bertha and her delicate, powdery skin? Yeah, we don't want that.

11. Too much shimmer. A little fairy dust on young girls or glitter on the tweeners is pretty and sparkly and young. Shimmer says, "Look at me!" After fifty, on our faces, it says, "Look at me, with sparkles in my lines! Can you see them *now*?" In our hair, it says, "Look at me, I'm thinning!" Above our boobs, it yells out, "Hey, check it out! I'm way down here now!"

So the next time you go to the Macy's or Nordstrom cosmetics department, jump up in a chair and let someone pamper you with a new look. It can be fun. And you don't have to buy a thing if you don't want to.

Plus, the perfect new lipstick can solve a lot of life's problems.

CHAPTER 9

You Said What?
26 Things Your Wife Never Wants to Hear

"Here's all you need to know about men and women: Women are crazy, men are stupid. And the main reason women are crazy is that men are stupid."
—George Carlin

HUBS AND I WERE GOING OUT with a group of friends for drinks at our favorite local restaurant, and I came out of the bedroom feeling all date-night in an off-the-shoulder fitted sweater with soft, slouchy jeans and fabulous boots.

Hubs pointed at my jeans and asked, with a slight frown, "What are those?"

"They're called boyfriend jeans," I replied.

"Are they supposed to fit like that?" he persisted, looking confused.

"Yes," I said, slowly. "That's why they're called *boyfriend* jeans. They're supposed to look like you're wearing your boyfriend's jeans."

Hubs waited a long moment and sealed their fate with, "Oh. Okay. But I'm kind of surprised that anyone who cares as much as you do about what your butt looks like would wear those jeans."

How many wrong things can one man say in one sentence?

Later, at the restaurant, I replayed the conversation with our group. The women began enthusiastically swapping hilarious stories of "Can you *believe* he said that?" until the men threw up their hands, insisting that women would be easier to communicate with if we came with a list of what they were never supposed to say.

We're glad you asked.

1. Oh, crap. Is today our anniversary? So not only did you forget, you find it *annoying*? Whatever you were thinking of buying her, get two.

2. Yes, I agree, your sister is totally hot. Never, *ever* tell us you've looked at Sissy in those terms. "I've never noticed" is the only acceptable response to this question.

3. You remind me of my ex when you do that. Oh, you mean the woman you've been referring to for the last decade as a bitchy, gold-digging tramp? You might want to consider flowers.

4. That's okay. I like a fuller-figured gal. OMG. "Fuller-figured," to every woman in every country on the planet, means *fat*. This one will require flowers *and* wine.

5. What did you do all day? The not-so-subtle implication being, "Did you sit on your lazy ass and watch TV all day, because it doesn't look like anything has been done around here." Are you *trying* to pick a fight?

6. If you want to go on a diet, I'll support you all the way. And *especially* if she didn't suggest the original idea. If she chooses to go on a diet and mentions it to you, the proper response is always, "Why? You're gorgeous."

7. Can't you take a joke? Usually used when you've just made one at her expense. It's a passive-aggressive way of taking a shot at her, but with plausible deniability. And she will *never* find it funny when you announce that the only way you can tell if you're getting laid is when she shaves her legs.

8. Have you taken your meds today? This is the boomer version of "Are you on your period?" Maybe we are or maybe we aren't. We're still going postal on your ass.

9. What did you do to your hair? There's not a woman alive who's going to interpret this as "Wow, you look great!" We hear, "When are you going to fix whatever you did to your hair?"

10. Are you going to eat all that? Translation: She eats like a linebacker. And from now on, she'll continue to eat whatever she likes. It just won't be while she's with *you*.

11. *Now* what's wrong? The implication being that she's impossible to please. You just threw a tank of gas on the fire.

12. Maybe you should ask my mother for her recipe. Yeah, just what every woman wants to hear: Mom did it better.

13. Is that your third glass of wine? Counting a woman's drinks has never, in the history of alcohol, resulted in her drinking less. And in about thirty minutes, she's going to be drunk *and* pissed.

14. Is that what you're wearing? Guaranteed to make you late for wherever you're going, because she's going up to change her clothes. Nine times.

15. You look fine. "Fine" is how you describe flooring and whether or not it needs to be replaced. Fine means, "not great, but we're running late, so let's *go*."

16. You knew I was like this when you married me. Well, that was twenty-two years ago, and she was kind of hoping you'd grow out of it someday.

17. You're not *that* old. Semi-witty references to her passing years will not be perceived as funny or complimentary. "You'll always be beautiful to me" is the safest response to comments about her midlife years. But for the love of God, do *not* add "no matter what."

18. You look tired. You may as well just tell her she looks like crap. Yeah, *that* will make her feel better.

19. You need to calm down. Visualize throwing the cat into the hot tub. That's what she's going to look like in three, two, one...

20. Why don't you ever wear clothes like that? As in, "Why don't you ever look that hot?" If I have to explain this one, you're probably better off single.

21. Get off my back. She hears, "You're a nag. Go away and leave me alone." Be careful with this one. One day, she might not come back.

22. It was just a kiss. There's No. Such. Thing.

23. What were you *thinking*? Man-speak for, "You're a complete idiot, and *no one* has ever done anything this stupid." Her response is likely to be, "I know. It's the second stupidest thing I've ever done." Guess which was the first?

24. Whatever. Dismissive and condescending, she hears, "This conversation is over." That may be true, but the conversation you're about to have *about* this conversation is going to be a doozy.

25. Technically, we were still married, but... If you plan to stay married to this woman (or ever want to have sex with her again), *stop talking*. There is no way to end this sentence and save the marriage. Many men have tried. None have succeeded.

26. No. 'Nuf said.

CHAPTER 10

A 50ᵗʰ Birthday, Menopause, and an Empty Nest.
Are We DONE Yet?

"We're adults. When did that happen? How do we make it stop?"
—Dr. Meredith Grey, *Grey's Anatomy*

2006 WAS A MOMENTOUS YEAR. I turned fifty, menopause was tap dancing all over my body, and just when I thought I had a handle on things, my only child moved out.

As for birthdays, I loved turning thirty. It sounded mature and sophisticated.

Turning forty was *fun*. I was still healthy and attractive (if you're grading on a curve), and there was still time to do the things on my bucket list.

Then came fifty.

Fifty kicked my ass. I gained ten pounds in my sleep, and my new menopausal metabolism now meant I had to limit my daily caloric intake to what would sustain a gerbil and join a gym *right freakin' now* because crucial body parts were migrating south at an alarming rate, apparently never to return without concentrated effort or surgical intervention. Awesome.

Menopause lasted for *years*, and Hubs started wearing fleece pj's eight months out of the year, as I repeatedly ran through the house opening all the windows, yelling, *"IT'S TOO DAMN HOT IN HERE."* When I insisted we keep the air-conditioning on year-round, he began to refer to our bedroom as "that meat locker we sleep in."

And, of course, there were the seismic mood swings, which invariably sent the Chihuahuas diving under the beds and the family scrambling for cover in any room I wasn't in.

Then, that same year, somewhere between the overnight weight gain and the next hot flash, my only child moved out, having registered for college *and* enlisting in the National Guard, which included a year-long deployment to Iraq. I was intensely proud of him. I also cried for a week.

It's not that I think that offspring should never leave the nest and get an adult life. That's normal, healthy, and as it should be. But when you're the mama being left behind, it's life-altering. I had to come to terms with the fact that my life been irrevocably changed.

When my son was very young, I realized quickly that I was never going to be a "regular mom." I don't do macaroni art, I don't have the patience for making Halloween costumes, and my bake sale goodies were always store-bought.

My job as his mom was less about making papier-mâché volcanoes on my dining table and more about keeping him *safe* and in his happy bubble, surrounded by unicorns and rainbows as much as possible. He was my boy, and my primary purpose was to stand between him and anyone or anything that could ever cause him pain.

Experts often say that we should let our kids experience disappointment, failure, frustration, and even a broken heart or two. They claim it teaches them compassion and empathy. I say those experts are idiots. This was my *baby*. I wasn't about to sit back and watch some pony-tailed mean girl from the local high school do a tap dance on his heart or do nothing while a bully, posing as a teacher, told my son he'd "never amount to much." Not. Going. To. Happen.

Of course, protecting someone requires information that's often extremely difficult to get. If you have teenage boys, you already know it's virtually impossible to get a boy cub to dish about his *real day*. And the stuff they won't tell you is *exactly* what you need to know.

One weekend while he was staying with friends, Hubs and I did a sweep of his bedroom. We needed information, and this was one very closed teenager. He told us *nothing*. So we decided to take a moment for some parental exploring in the great abyss known as a teenager's bedroom. Forty-five minutes later, we'd found enough clues to piece together the path he was on and who the key players were.

Young grasshopper, big surprise, wasn't wild about the "No Privacy" laws of the house. I assured him that he'd understand some day if he ever had a boy. He now has a six-year-old son. I told him to call me in ten years, and we'll walk him through the room sweep.

Over the years, I've tossed out his phone because his friends on speed dial were iffy at best. I taught him how to extricate himself from a relationship without putting the girl in therapy and helped him write more letters and fill in more applications than his high school guidance counselor. He frequently asked my advice. It was a wonderful time, and I felt needed and relevant.

Then he married a beautiful young woman, and they became a family with two small children. For months, I watched as he naturally found his own way as a husband, a father, and a military officer, while going to college full time. I was home, struggling with my changing relationship with my only child and wondering what my role would be.

I vowed daily never to be one of those mothers who called her son every day or insisted he call her weekly so she knows every detail of her grown child's life. His life was now separate from mine, and I just had to wait for my place to unfold.

Then one day, he called. "Mom, I need help with my college loan applications." And then another. "The boy is acting out. What should we do?" And yet another. "Will you help me with my résumé?" This pattern continued, and is still in place to this day.

I felt like Sally Field, only I was shouting "He needs me! He really, really needs me!" I've become the Git 'er Done mom to whom my adult child turns when something needs to happen, preferably *now*. I'm thinking of ordering some business cards that say, "The Go-To Mom, For When You Want to Get Shit *Done*."

I can live with that.

CHAPTER 11

Age-Appropriate Style.
It's Not Just About Your Mother Anymore.

"If high heels were so wonderful, men would still be wearing them."
—Sue Grafton

I REMEMBER THE FIRST TIME I was called "ma'am." I also remember finally being called "Grandma." And I clearly remember when I exchanged showing my ID to order a drink with showing my ID for the senior discount.

But none of those moments made me feel as old as the first time I ventured out of a department store dressing room in a new dress and the tweener salesclerk smiled brightly and chirped, "You look great! And you can wear it anywhere, because it's, like, *totally* age appropriate."

Age appropriate? Listen up, Twinkie. I'm way too young to be worrying about "age appropriate" clothing. That's for our mothers. Today's grandmas still rock skinny jeans and stilettos. Toss me a pair of thigh-length Spanx and the tube dress on that mannequin over there, and I'll show you how it's *done,* Baby Girl.

But on the walk of shame back to my dressing room, I started thinking about longstanding fashion rules for women, many of which have been generally dismissed over the years as we collectively discovered that the world doesn't actually care if we wear white after Labor Day or mix red and pink together in the same outfit. Rules were made to be broken, and female baby boomers are exploding fashion rules every day.

Unfortunately, in our youth-obsessed society, with beauty pageants for six-year-old girls and college students getting tummy tucks, our definition of "age appropriate" has become a bit blurry.

We start questioning our wardrobes, asking ourselves, "Is this too young for me?" Or we see another fifty-something woman in a leopard-print skirt and wince, thinking, "I have that skirt. Do I *look* like that?" The rules have been tossed out, and now we're no longer certain what works and what doesn't after a certain age.

The good news? While there are no hard-and-fast rules, there are a few guidelines to help you navigate the landmine of dressing young when you're... well... *not*. It's easier than you think. Simply put, your clothes need to match your face. Avoid the following:

1. Cutsie Betty Boop, Hello Kitty, Mickey Mouse or other Disney attire. By fifty, you need to look like a grownup.

2. Fad pieces that don't work for your body. This would include rompers and low-rise sweatpants with "Juicy" emblazoned in neon across your butt.

3. Miniskirts. Unless you're at a karaoke bar, belting out a rocking Tina Turner rendition of "Proud Mary," miniskirts after fifty say, "Hey sailor, looking for a good time?"

4. Message T-shirts. "Still a Bad Ass" and "Sexy Grandma" written across boobs that are now closer to your waist than your clavicle bone is just *wrong*.

5. Short-shorts. They looked trashy on Daisy Duke. And she was a twenty-two-year-old gazelle. Don't even think about it.

6. Plunging necklines. Our boobs are already plunging. Do we need to advertise it?

7. Jeans with rhinestones. Ditto rhinestone baseball caps. Or anything bedazzled. And that includes your vajayjay.

8. Extremely low-rise jeans. The color of your underwear, the fact that you don't wear underwear, or the exact starting point of your butt crack should stay between you and whoever actually asks to see it. The rest of us prefer to simply speculate. Or not.

9. Stupid shoes. Thigh-high boots (outside of the bedroom), knee-high gladiator sandals, platform sneakers. What works for Madonna on stage can make the average fifty-something boomer on the street look like a transvestite with no taste.

10. Little-girl hair accessories. Sweet barrettes, bows, and rhinestone headbands. If your three-year-old granddaughter wants it, give it to her. For keeps. (See #1).

11. Anything purchased at Forever 21. Or Claire's. Or any store where the salesgirl uses "like" before every third word.

12. Too much sexy (yes, it's possible). Despite what Hubs thinks, four-inch stilettos, a short skirt, and a strapless top, worn simultaneously (even if they all fit and you can walk in the shoes), makes you look slutty, not sexy.

13. Anything that looks better on your DIL than on you. If it requires perky boobs, flat, non-child-bearing abs, cellulite-free thighs, or triceps you could bounce a quarter from, and *this no longer describes you*, pass it along to the next generation.

14. Anything you've had in your closet for over ten years. I know it was expensive and you love it. But in ten years, styles evolve. Hopefully, so have you. Let it go.

Having said all that, I'm *not* a 24/7 fashionista. While I love getting "all done up," as Hubs would say, I'm equally comfortable in the ubiquitous yoga pants and T-shirt ensemble that female boomers have adopted as the uniform of our generation, especially while living in a small town with a very relaxed fashion culture.

I was out running a few errands recently, so it was just a quick shower, some workout gear (more YMCA than Bali Fitness), no makeup, and out the door.

On the third stop, I ran into an old friend, all skinny jeans, bangles, full makeup, and gorgeous hair. I frantically tried to hide behind the zucchini counter, but no such luck. After air kisses and mutual exclamations of "It's been *so* long! You look GREAT!" she smiled ever-so-sweetly and said, "You know what I've always *loved* about you?"

"Do tell," I replied, instinctively sensing I wasn't going to like what came next.

"You're so *real*," she gushed. "You can get all dressed up and look fabulous, of course, but you're just as comfortable going out like…" She waved her hand in my general direction. "Well… *this*."

My mother always taught me to answer compliments with a simple and gracious "Thank you," which I managed to choke out, but I kept thinking it was a good thing she didn't see me last Thursday at Safeway in my jammies. I'd never leave home again.

CHAPTER 12
28 Best Momisms About Beauty

"When your mother asks, 'Do you want a piece of advice?' it's merely a formality. You're going to get it anyway."
—Erma Bombeck

MY MOTHER WAS A MILF. Of course, she didn't know it at the time. It was, after all, in the 1960s, and MILFs were officially forty-plus years down the road. When I was in my teens, she would have been referred to as "hot" or "a fox." Suffice it to say, she was stunning, and all my teenage boyfriends loved her.

Mom grew up in the '50s. She was slender, wasp-waisted, with a perfect, blonde beehive hairdo, and smelled like Youth Dew from Estee Lauder. She wore slim skirts and stilettos, and always "freshened up" by fixing her hair and makeup before Dad came home. This was not a home that fostered tomboys. My sister and I grew up, not surprisingly, to be girly-girls, with a love of fashion, makeup, and all things beautiful.

Sissy and I learned very early that beauty was *work*. One had to *pay attention*, so nothing slipped through the cracks and identified us as "lazy" or "tacky" or, worst of all, like we came from the "Squattley family." (Nobody ever actually met a Squattley, but you didn't want to be mistaken for one. Ever.)

Beauty came with *rules,* and Mom knew exactly how to deliver them with the conviction of Moses reading the Stone Tablets. With six kids at home (three hers and three his), she had no time for chatty mother-daughter discussions and lessons on how not to disgrace ourselves and ruin the family name for future generations. Mom had a quick, dry wit and a scathing sense of humor, and she delivered most of her advice on the fly. One-liners or pithy instructions would spring forth spontaneously at home, in the car, or in the produce department of the local supermarket. At a young age, I learned to carry a pencil and a notepad in anticipation of her sidelong glance that told me *something I needed to know* was forthcoming.

By the time we were in our teens, Sissy and I had memorized The Rules through repeated daily reminders from our personal Beauty Sherpa. Some have been easier to follow than others, and a few are now more relevant to an earlier time, but at seventy-plus and still fabulous, Mom has a certain credibility that can't be denied.

1. You have to suffer to be beautiful. I learned this one at fourteen, while getting braces put on my teeth. Forty-plus years later, it's about stilettos, Spanx, skinny jeans, and Botox injections. Some truths never change.

2. At a certain age, a woman has to choose between her face and her ass. Skinny older women look even older. And they're cranky. Eat. (Bless you, Mom.)

3. The difference between a beautiful woman and an ugly woman is either God or a ton of money.

4. Beauty comes from within, but the outside needs a little makeup. And a good bra.

5. If you must smoke, do so only while seated. Walking with a cigarette makes you look like a Squattley.

6. If you think you're fat, you probably are.

7. If you're wider from the side view than from the front view, you're definitely fat.

8. Walk lightly, and don't tromp. You're a girl, not a Clydesdale.

9. When a man insists he likes his wife "natural," without makeup or any visible effort, you can bet his mistress is anything but.

10. If you drink, do so in moderation. Drunk is never a woman's best presentation. (Mom always insisted that if a woman could see herself on video while drunk, she'd never make that mistake again. YouTube would agree.)

11. A woman is instantly judged by her shoes and her handbag. Economize somewhere else.

12. If you paint your nails, no chips. If you color your hair, no roots. It looks cheap. (She thought the ombre hair color fad was just plain stupid, and we almost lost her during the grunge era.)

13. If you keep frowning, your face will freeze like that. (Fortunately, Botox freezes it back.)

14. Don't curse. It makes you sound like a trucker, and only a certain type of man wants a trucker.

15. Keep your nails short. Men find long red nails scary. A woman can't have long red nails *and* a good sex life.

16. Men are visual. That's why they like stilettos. And porn. That's also why they don't need to see you toileting, plucking your brows, or shaving anything but your legs.

17. Stand up straight. It projects confidence. Besides, hunching makes your boobs look droopy.

18. Never chew gum. People who chew gum look like cows chewing cud.

19. Know how to be a lady. If you want to be a tramp, do it in the bedroom, but you should *always* be a lady in public.

20. Whenever you're trying to change something about yourself, be realistic. Only God can make a tree.

21. A woman has the face God gave her at twenty and the face she's earned at fifty. Wear sunscreen. And don't squint.

22. Learn to walk in stilettos, even if only in the bedroom. Men love them. Always have, always will. Get used to it.

23. Be careful when wearing prints, especially on the bottom. Nobody ever looked at the wrong end of a zebra and said, "Wow. That zebra sure has a tiny ass."

24. Be sparing with cosmetic intervention. Your face should never look younger than the rest of you.

25. When your makeup is done and you're ready to go out, take half of it off. Less is more.

26. Look good when your husband gets home, and look happy to see him. If you don't, someone else will.

27. Get your hair off of your face. You look like a sheepdog.

28. SMILE. It's the most beautiful thing you can wear.

Thanks, Mom, for these pearls of female wisdom over the years. Some make me think. Others still make me snort-laugh out loud (which I know is terribly unladylike). But most of these have stood the test of time, and I'll be passing them along to my granddaughter when she's ready. Until then, I don't chew gum, but I still can't master those damn stilettos.

CHAPTER 13

It's Swimsuit Season. Pass the Milk Duds.

"Midlife brings the wisdom that life throws you curves. You're now sitting on your biggest ones."
—Unknown

ENJOYING THE WARMER temperatures and anticipating upcoming spring weather, I took a look at my all-black closet and decided to go do some spring shopping for a little color. My plans took a slight shift when Hubs unexpectedly announced he'd like to join me. But then I envisioned a few new purchases with a stop for a glass of yummy red wine at whatever outdoor café (okay, bar) that we found along the way, so we hopped in the car and headed for Portland.

Scratching my original plans for a leisurely, day-long stroll through my favorite boutiques (Hubs's shopping style is more "get in, buy it, get out"), we hit the mall. Lights, noise, food courts, and miles of brightly-lit windows featuring hot colors, shorter lengths, and summer fabrics.

We found a store we liked; I grabbed a few colorful pieces and a swimsuit then happily headed for the dressing room, imagining my trendy summer style. Fifteen minutes later, the day was going south on a luge. The cute pink jeans wouldn't budge past my thighs. *Seriously?* I peeled them off and checked the size. Yep, size eight. Apparently that refers to my *knees*, not my hips, because those suckers weren't going all the way up in this lifetime.

Tossed them over the swinging door in a disgusted heap and grabbed the shorts. (Yeah, *there's* a good idea: if the jeans don't fit, try the shorts.) Hopped up and down, trying to heave-*ho* them up far enough to button the waist until I finally squeezed the snap shut.

Oh. My. God. I looked like a giant banana-nut muffin. And when did my thighs start jiggling? They didn't jiggle *last* year. But there they were, in all their white, tanless glory, shaking like jello shots to the beat of "Girls Just Wanna Have Fun" blaring over the loudspeaker, which wouldn't have been so depressing if I hadn't been *standing still.*

I looked up to see Hubs poking his head over the door and smiling. "I found a few pair of jeans for myself while I was waiting."

"Did you try them on?" I asked.

"Don't need to. They're a 36. They'll be fine."

"Hating you just a little bit right now."

In my final act of desperation, I grabbed the swimsuit (one-piece, skirted bottom, very '40s pin-up retro, and *black*... Could work). Size eight to ten? Yeah, if you live in Taiwan and your fit model is a twelve-year-old *boy.* I looked like a wiener dog stuffed into a tube top, with skin squishing out at both ends.

By then I was in tears, and Hub was calling through the door, "Is there anything I can get for you, sweetie?"

"A hankie," I sniffled. And a gun.

Meanwhile, the fourteen-year-old anorexic salesgirl with impossibly long, *firm* legs chirped out, "Don't worry, ma'am." (*ma'am?*) "It's not summer yet. You still have time." *To do what?* Lose the same ten pounds I've been working on since 1974? *Oh, shut up and go eat a cheeseburger.*

We bought Hubs's new jeans and left my dressing room piled high with tiny little clothing pieces in a size I obviously no longer wore, along with the last shred of my dignity. On our way to the winery, Hubs suggested a quick stop at Safeway for a few essentials.

At day's end, you've got to love a man who watches you toss Milk Duds, Hot Tamales, Fig Newtons, ice cream sandwiches, Lucky Charms, and half a dozen bottles of wine (10% off with six!) into the cart, while wailing the entire time about how *hard* it is to lose weight, *and* who has the good grace (and natural survival skills) Not. To. Say. A. Word.

CHAPTER 14

13 Reasons I Couldn't be Married to Me

"Women are meant to be loved, not to be understood."
—Oscar Wilde

ON OUR ANNIVERSARY THIS YEAR, Hubs gave me a beautiful, oversize card that listed a few of my better qualities and why Hallmark thought he'd scored when we got married. As I was reading it, I found myself mentally rewriting the card with reasons he didn't get quite so lucky but chose to stick it out anyway, which is actually a better love story.

As I was jotting down an embarrassingly-long list of my less-than-stellar characteristics that would deter all but the most hardy partner, he looked over my shoulder with a big grin, saying, "This is *great*. If you need more, I can add several off the top of my head." One look at the expression on my face, and, not being a stupid man, he immediately added, "But they wouldn't all necessarily be *true*, of course." Nice save, buddy.

An hour or so later, he was red-faced from laughing, while I was trying desperately to retain the tiniest shred of self-esteem, and we'd compiled a fairly impressive list. So, with a little help (and considerably more enthusiasm than the discussion required) from Hubs, here are the "14 Reasons I Couldn't Be Married to Me."

1. I'm undiagnosed but collectively believed by family, friends, and a couple of ex-husbands to be OCD *and* ADHD. My last husband frequently remarks that I don't get divorced so much as I just leave my husbands in exhausted heaps on the side of the road as what he calls "the empty carcasses of the men they used to be."

2. I'm not a nurturer. If you're sick, I'll take your dog to the groomer, pick up your dry-cleaning, or feed your gerbil. But you'll never hear the words, "Oh my poor Pookey Bear, let me feed you this homemade soup" come out of my mouth. *Ever*.

3. I tend to burst out laughing at the most inopportune times, when virtually any other response would be a better choice. Like when we're fighting. Or during sex. "I'm not laughing *at* you, but *with* you" gets a lot of play time at our house.

4. I'm easily frustrated. If I can't do something after two tries, it's most likely been tossed out the window into the soccer field next door. It's our version of a garage sale, but everything is free.

5. I can't cook. At all. When we got our first microwave (yes, a billion years ago), I put a peanut butter sandwich in it to warm it up, set the timer for fifteen minutes, and went to take a shower. When I returned, the door had blown open, showering cupboards and countertops with bits of exploded sandwich pieces, and we were scraping bits of peanut butter, jelly, and/or bread off canned goods for a week. My skills have never improved.

6. I have no filter. Hubs asks, with only slightly annoying regularity, "Do you *think* before you speak, or do you just open your mouth and let the words fall out?" Yeah, the second one.

7. I don't share my food. With three older brothers, two dads, and a couple of ex-husbands who all seemed to think that my plate looked more appetizing than theirs and believed that anything less than half a serving still constitutes "just a bite," I've learned to guard my dinner by threatening to stab a fork through any hand found hovering over my plate.

8. I don't always listen, regularly replying before Hubs has stopped speaking. He calls it interrupting. I call it enthusiasm.

9. I have the attention span of a circus flea for things I'm not interested in. Hubs gave up by our second year of trying to get me into televised sports, and the 130th replay of his golf stroke on Hole #9 will most likely send me running for the corkscrew and second bottle of wine.

10. I have pretty much zero fears about failure. Not because I don't fail, but because it doesn't faze me. Epic fails make great dinner conversation, especially with your kids, and then become your best blog posts. People may or may not want to hear about your successful weight loss or how much you give to charity every year, but they're all over the time you drove over the neighbor's previously prize-winning cat's tail wearing nothing but your underwear.

11. I constantly whine about my weight but continue to fill our grocery cart with food items not recognized by any diet program anywhere on the planet. Hubs has learned not to say a word.

12. I spend stupid amounts of money on products that promise to make me thinner, prettier, or younger, especially if they require minimal to no effort on my part. I don't see this pattern diminishing as I get even older.

13. I don't like to fight, but if you insist, your cousin Beauford, his banjo, and his whiskey-loving goat are fair game.

Personally, I'd drop-kick this woman's ass to the door. But for some unfathomable reason, Hubs keeps coming home every night. As we reviewed our list, he grinned and said, "You're kind of one of those 'Be Careful What You Wish For' things." Then he grabbed a blank sheet of paper, scribbled on it for a few minutes, and handed it to me with a flourish. "Here's your *real* card."

The front said, *I asked God to send me a woman who makes me laugh.* The inside read, *Clearly, I should have been a bit more specific.* Then he said the Big Guy whispered in his ear, "Done. She's at the airport. But no refunds and no exchanges. My phone line is always open, however. Good luck, buddy, and just remember—this was *your* idea."

And they lived happily ever after.

CHAPTER 15
Pee Test…You're Doing it Wrong

"I'm not offended by dumb blonde jokes because I know I'm not dumb, and I'm also not blonde."
—Dolly Parton

LIVING ON MAUI for several years was truly an adventure. There are many cultural idiosyncrasies, and one of them is the thoroughness with which they check you out before they hire you for virtually *any* job.

Since many people move to the Islands specifically to escape (literally or figuratively) from the mainland and become more "one with the universe" (with the first order of business often being a name change from Brunhilde Rabinowitz, stock girl at WalMart in Dayton, Ohio, to Summer Rain, numerologist and chakra reader under the waterfalls of Kula) it behooves employers to dig up a little more information than simply taking your word for who you are and what's written on your new, fantasy résumé.

Having worked in retail since, basically, *ever*, I applied for a position of store manager at an upscale Hawaiian boutique. The interview and background check went well, so my next stop was the local Klinika for pre-employment drug screening, universally known as the "pee test." Never having been pee-tested before and not sure what they were looking for, I had even given up wine while I was job hunting. (Oh sure, *now* I know that they wouldn't test a forty-year-old for alcohol, but I was new at this; I wasn't taking any chances.)

I piled my seven-year-old son into the car and drove to the small, island-type structure staffed by five or six Hawaiian women in hibiscus-printed nurse's outfits. One of them smiled and asked why I was there. Before I could say a word, The Boy looked up and announced, "Mommy's here so you can check her for drugs!" Then he leaned forward and loudly whispered, "And she even quit drinking last week!" *Thanks, honey.* Now the entire place thinks I'm in AA. That sound you hear is my career going down in flames of palm fronds.

The nurse smiled and handed me a little yellow cup, all bound up with what looked like an entire roll of duct tape and a large key attached to it, and pointed me to a small room, where I spent the next twenty minutes peeling miles of sticky duct tape off the container (geez, I'd heard they were tamper-proof, but this was *ridiculous*), until I *finally* unwrapped the lid, did my duty for God and King Kamehameha, then spent *another* 20 minutes re-taping the damn thing before triumphantly returning with my sample to the front desk, at which point the entire staff burst into hysterical, raucous laughter.

At my confused expression, the nurse wiped her eyes and gleefully choked out, between bouts of uncontrollable mirth, "Thanks, Blondie, but your container is on the shelf. You just peed in our key ring. I've been here sixteen years, and nobody's *ever* done that before! Lady, we'll be telling this story for *years!*"

Dear Lord, if there really is a Rapture, suck me up now.

CHAPTER 16
50. How Not to Make it the New 75

"The heyday of a woman's life is the shady side of fifty."
—Elizabeth Cady Stanton

IT SEEMS LIKE I'M CONSTANTLY stumbling across references to "The New 50." "50 is the new 40" articles and posters crop up online and on Facebook seemingly by the minute, assuring us to whom it matters that we may *be* fifty-something, but we can *look* forty-something. Not as easy as it sounds.

For many of us, our fifties are a time when we begin to struggle with issues that seem to have cropped up overnight. (I *swear* I gained ten pounds the day I turned fifty, and they've permanently parked themselves across my midsection with the tenacity of chewing gum in a toddler's hair.) Suddenly, phrases like "age-appropriate" filter into our clothes shopping, makeup we've worn forever now looks somehow wrong, and we're wondering if we should grow our super-short hair into a more flattering length but aren't quite sure what that is.

Having been in the retail beauty business since the invention of lip gloss, I've learned that the best source of beauty advice is, not surprisingly, *other women*. Women are wonderfully willing to share insider secrets and tips, and I've yet to meet a beautiful woman who has tired of being asked how exactly she got that way. I've collected dozens of tips over the years on how to age well, and what I've learned is that what you *don't* do is as important as what you *do*. So I'm sharing with you my most-repeated advice from gorgeous women who have shared it with me (because I'm generous that way).

Top 10 Things to Avoid, to Not Look Old:

1. Mom jeans. High-waisted, tapered or cropped at the ankle, and made of heavy denim that adds the equivalent of a backwards fanny pack directly on the belly, where most of us need it the least. You don't need to pay $175 for flattering jeans, but you do need to shop at stores that don't sell power tools and doggie kibble one aisle over from the sports bras.

2. Bad bras. Ill-fitted, with not enough support for two M&Ms, much less gravity-assaulted beagle ears. By your fifties, it's time to start buying bras that actually fit and that get 'em *up* there. Keep the lacy, dental-floss styles for the bedroom.

3. Overdone makeup. Heavy foundation falls into the cracks, red lipstick bleeds, and thick eyeliner starts looking a little "Elvira, Mistress of the Dark." Lighten up. You'll look years younger and your pillowcases won't look like a four-color Rorschach test every morning.

4. Mall hair. If your bangs resemble a large cauliflower floret attached to the center of your forehead, it's time to rethink your stylist. I'm not sure why hair schools teach that unfortunate cut, but they must, because it's *everywhere* in rural America. Bangs should not look like they sprouted from your forehead independently of the rest of your hair.

5. Baggy, oversize clothes. If you could fit a ham hock up under your shirt, I guarantee you that you look heavier and older than your years. Baggy clothes don't hide middle-age weight gain. They draw attention to it by suggesting you're actually filling up all that space. Think maternity clothes. What woman *ever* looked thinner in anything called a "smock"? Find a style that flatters your shape, and then buy every color they make.

6. Conversely, your daughter's clothes. This is the epitome of "Just because you can, doesn't mean you should." Yippee for you (and I mean that; really, I do) that you're fifty-five and still wear a size two, but this does not give you free rein to root through your size-two, seventeen-year-old daughter's closet for what to wear to your high school reunion. Trust me: everyone will know how tiny you still are, even without the midriff-baring top and the vagina-peeking skirt.

7. No sunscreen. Very few things turn our faces into the backside of a saddlebag faster than sun exposure. Wear a minimum of 15 SPF. Every. Single. Day. And don't be saying, "Well, I use sunscreen in the summer." Swell, except that 80% of premature aging comes from UVA rays: the year-round ones that cut through clouds and glass; that we're exposed to when we go out to get the mail. In February. And for those of you still using tanning beds... *STOP THAT!*

8. Church Lady clothes. Skirts longer than your vajayjay doesn't mean a drab A-line down to your mid-calf, and less cleavage doesn't mean buttoned up to your upper clavicle with a white Peter Pan collar and matching self-belt. If Laura Ingalls Wilder wore it to church on *Little House, you* shouldn't be wearing it, *ever.* If you're not sure what length works for you, grab a well-dressed girlfriend to go shopping with you and agree to try on *every single thing* she brings you. You'll both have a ball.

9. Too thin. I added this one because I love you. Yep, too thin can be aging. The body and face need a little padding to soften lines and smooth the skin, making us look healthier and (there is a God) younger. So have a piece of cheesecake. And a glass of wine. Your face will thank you.

10. Woman on Top. My Grammy, whose pithy wisdom I still miss every day, instructed me years ago to grab a large mirror and lay it on the floor, then kneel over it on all fours. Look down. That's what your partner sees when you're on top. (Go ahead and try it. We'll wait.) If your face skin falls forward like a TV ad for the Lifestyle Lift®, or your boobs dangle like two sock puppets on a clothes line and your belly drops low enough to sway to the beat, it's time to get underneath or consider dimming the lights. Hubs and I have been doing it in the dark since I was in my forties. He blames it on childhood nightmares. He has no idea.

CHAPTER 17
I'm at Grandma's. Dial 9-1-1

"My grandmother started walking five miles a day when she was 60. She's 97 now, and we don't know where the hell she is."
—Ellen DeGeneres

MY SON CALLED TO SAY that they were bringing the grandkids for the weekend. Yay! Upon their arrival, he and Hubs immediately took off for Home Depot for some manly-man errands (conveniently located directly across from their favorite sports bar... Yeah, they were gone for the day). DIL and I got the wee ones occupied then we settled in for giggles and gossip.

Sometime later, I noticed my five-year-old grandson was not where I'd left him. Not panicking quite yet, we set off to search the house. He was nowhere to be found.

Okay, *now* we're panicking.

We spent the next forty-five minutes tearing the house apart, running down the street, knocking on doors, and searching the soccer field across the street. No signs of him. By this time, DIL was hysterical and I was getting ready to call 9-1-1, when we heard the sound of angels... a thumping from the trunk of their car and a little voice yelling, "Grandma, here I am!"

After hugs and tears and a giant bowl of ice cream for the little guy, who was ever so proud of his secret hiding place where "even Mommy and Grandma couldn't find me!" we gently explained to young grasshopper that mommies and grandmas don't particularly *like* hide-and-seek, and we didn't want to play that game *EVER AGAIN.*

By Sunday, I was comatose on the couch. Three full, busy days with Hubs, me, our son, his wife, little guy, his new baby sister, their puppy, our two Chihuahuas, *and* my ex-husband, who 'd flown in from Maui to see the kids (yes, he stays with us… it's weird, but it works).

Sleeping bags and air mattresses in the living room; nonstop laundry; grandson meltdown because he lost his first tooth and promptly swallowed it, inconsolable because that meant the tooth fairy wouldn't come; a Grandma-lesson in why she shouldn't put her wine in a bright yellow plastic cup and set it within arm's reach of grandson, proving that grandson has a prematurely sophisticated palette and likes Cabernet, but not scoring any points with prodigy's parents; granddaughter constantly looking for milk boobs like a shark for fish (even with Grandma, no matter how many times I told her mine weren't functional… Hell, they're barely decorative anymore); three yappy alpha dogs Scooby-doo'ing across the hardwood in nonstop chase mode (one pooped on my best area rug, but the other two aren't giving him up… Oh sure, *now* they're friends); kitchen set continually on "graze," with dishes to match; and toys, porta-cribs, diaper bags, car seats, and video games covering every surface of the house.

As they were all loading up their cars and I was gazing longingly at my fluffy down comforter and king-size bed, my daughter-in-law looked at me and laughed. "But if we told you we were all coming back next weekend, you'd love it."

And she's right.

CHAPTER 18

The 12 Stupidest Love Songs, Ever

"I don't want to be in love, but you're making me."
—Jonny Lang

AS VALENTINE'S DAY LOOMS closer, retailers are blanketing the shopping universe with cut-out hearts and chalky sugar treats emblazoned with "Be My Baby," designed to get us opening our wallets to share romantic, gift-laden evenings with our special someone. Valentine's Day is the great romantic do-over for those who dropped the ball at Christmas, sending couples scrambling once again to find the elusive perfect gift for Baby Cakes.

Valentine's Day gifts can be small and sentimental, or they can show up as white limo rides with a dozen red roses, á la *The Bachelor*. Whatever the actual gift might be, a little music can help set the mood. Whether it's used as background while exchanging coy I-love-you-No-I-love-you-more smiles over dinner for two, or as a dance to "our song," the music you choose can make or break the evening.

To help you narrow your search, I'm offering a list of what *NOT* to choose for your special Valentine's Day playlist. In no particular order of horribleness:

1. **Don't Know Much About History** (Sam Cooke). *"Don't know much about history, don't know much about biology."* Repeat for science, French, geography, trigonometry, algebra, and the nefarious slide rule. You get the idea. *"But if I could be with you, what a wonderful world it would be."* Seriously, dude? You just admitted to being on the wrong side of the Stupid bell curve, and yet somehow you think we're going to hook up and have a fab life together? Here's a thought. Get your GED, get a job, and lose my number.

2. **Better Dig Two** (Band Perry). *"I told you on the day we wed, I was gonna love you 'til I's dead. If the ties that bind ever do come loose, if 'forever' ever ends for you, read me my last rites. And let my stone say, Here lies a girl whose only crutch was loving one man a little too much. If you go before I do, gonna tell the gravedigger he better dig two."* Wow. A hundred years of mothers teaching daughters independence and dignity just got completely obliterated by one song.

3. **Marry You** (Bruno Mars). *"It's a beautiful night. We're looking for something dumb to do. Hey Baby, I think I want to marry you. Who cares if we're trashed, got a pocket full of cash. If we wake up and you wanna break up, that's cool. It was fun, girl."* Worst proposal *ever*. And who needs a pre-nup when you've got a twenty-four-hour annulment clause in your back pocket?

4. **Into the Night** (Benny Mardones). *"She's just sixteen years old…"* That also makes her illegal in pretty much all fifty states. Go find a grown-up, Bens.

5. **Ticks** (Brad Paisley). *"You press that bottle to your lips, and I wish I was your beer. The only thing allowed to crawl over you is me. You know every guy here would like to take you home, but I've got more class than that. I'd like to check you for ticks."* Everything people don't like about country music, all in one song. Go Brad.

6. **You Lie** (The Band Perry). *"You lie like a priceless Persian rug on a rich man's floor. You lie like a coon dog basked in the sunshine on my porch. You lie like a penny in the parking lot."* What do these even *mean*? Possibly the worst analogies in song-writing history.

7. **Two Out of Three Ain't Bad** (Meat Loaf). *"I want you, I need you, but there ain't no way I'm ever gonna love you. Now don't be sad, cuz two out of three ain't bad,"* followed by an entire verse lamenting the one that got away, but whom he never got over. Well, gee, Mr. Loaf. While I appreciate your only slightly arrogant offer and the assumption that I'd be grateful for two-thirds of your awesomeness, I think I'd rather date your ex-girlfriend.

8. **Having My Baby** (Paul Anka). *"Having my baby, what a lovely way of saying how much you love me."* Yeah, because this really is all about *you*, Paul. Then it gets tacky. *"Didn't have to keep it. You could've swept it from your life but you wouldn't do it."* Show of hands to anyone who doesn't know what Pauly is referring to. How much bad taste can one song encompass?

9. **Every Breath You Take** (Sting). *"Every breath you take, every move you make, every bond you break"* (insert more of the same) *"I'll be watching you."* Then you'll be watching me take out a restraining order on your stalker ass.

10. **Why Don't We Get Drunk** (Jimmy Buffett). Jimmy, Jimmy, Jimmy. What happened? *"I just bought a water bed. It's filled up for me and you. Yeah, now baby, why don't we get drunk and screw?"* I'm trying to imagine the target that this line would work on, and I can only assume she's a wide-eyed band groupie who thinks "banging" is a proper synonym for sex. Leave the twenty-somethings alone, Jimmy, and have another margarita.

11. **You Remind Me of Something** (R Kelly). And just when you thought all the bad lyrics were taken. *"You remind me of my Jeep, I wanna ride it. Something like my sound, I wanna pump it. You look just like my cars, I wanna wax it. And something like my bank account, I wanna spend it."* So you're saying you want to ride me, pump me, wax me, and spend me. *Uh,* okay. Should I shave my legs first?

And my all-time favorite...

12. **This Girl is a Woman Now** (Gary Puckett). *"This girl walked in dreams... This girl was a child... Then one night her world was changed"* (insert sex with Mr. Puckett) *"and she will never be the same again. This girl is a woman now. She's found out what it's all about, and she's learning to live."* Well, Mr. Puckett, those must be some damn fine lovemaking skills you've got. You took a girl and made a woman out of her. I'll bet her Daddy is just tickled pink. He was just spotted reloading at the local gun shop. You might want to move along now to a different house. Or a different state.

Now let's cuddle up and have a slow dance.

CHAPTER 19
My Husband Thinks I'm a Witch.
He Might be Right

"Don't Make Me Drop a House on You."
—Fiona Goode, *American Horror Story*

MY GRANDMOTHER WAS A WITCH. Not as in "nasty old bat," but as in "I can put a curse on you"-type witch. Seriously, you did *not* want to make this woman angry or unhappy. If you fell from her good graces, she'd put the "fie" on you, and bad things would begin to happen. The early stories my mother used to tell me about Grandma and some poor, unfortunate soul stupid enough to give her a hard time or tell her anything she didn't want to hear I'd assumed were amusing coincidences.

As the years went by, however, I saw a pattern emerge. Either Grammy really *was* a witch, or she should start buying lottery tickets, because whatever this woman wanted to happen happened. Grammy had a lot of health problems, including the fact that she was given to, shall we say, generous proportions. One idiot pup of a doctor told her, in no uncertain terms, that she was *fat* and needed to lose weight. At her next appointment, the receptionist told us that he was no longer working there and nobody had any idea where he'd gone. Just sayin'.

Whether she was or wasn't, in fact, a witch with supernatural powers to right her wrongs, I was crazy about her, and she felt the same about me. I spent a lot of time with her when I was a very young child, and I still remember her holding me and whispering, "Just remember. You're *just like me*."

I didn't tell Hubs about Grandma in our early years together. "Hi. My grandmother was a witch who liked to put evil curses on people she didn't like, instantly turning their lives to crap" didn't seem like promising dating material. Sort of like saying, "I can imitate any noise in the animal kingdom. Wanna hear?" Or "I love to talk like a pirate and answer every question with 'Ay-ay, Matey!'" Those people tend to go on a lot of first dates but quickly learn that "I'll call you" is date-speak for "Buh-bye, nut job." I always thought I'd break the Grandma stories to him gently, *after* he was too in love to run.

But early on in our marriage, Hubs concluded (for reasons I *swear* I don't know) that I possessed some sort of weird, cosmic, witchy power to mess with people who pissed me off. Whenever anything bad would happen to someone he knew had offended me in some way, he'd give me a long look and ask, "Did you have anything to do with that?" (Fortunately this was rare, so I always laughed it off, but I never actually *denied* it. Grammy always said it's good to hold a card or two up your sleeve.)

Last night, Hubs decided to commandeer the big living room TV for the *entire night* to watch what was looking like a nine-hour basketball game, knowing full well I hate televised sports, essentially banishing me down the hall to the unfinished end of the house to sit on a card-table chair and watch my little office TV, by myself, on a Friday night.

During the next several hours, he sliced his hand open while making his favorite weenie wraps, dropped and busted his brand new cell phone, accidentally locked his beloved Chihuahua in the master bedroom, forcing her to pee on the carpet, and finally shattered a full glass of red wine all over the kitchen floor, showering glass shards and dark red wine sprays *everywhere*.

By the third quarter, he came barreling into my little office. "Okay, *I give up*! We can watch *Grey's Anatomy*! Just *TAKE OFF THE DAMN CURSE*."

I just smiled sweetly and told him to finish the game, because that's the kind of good witch I am.

CHAPTER 20
The Reality Check. 10 Epic Fails

"People are giving birth underwater now. They say it's less traumatic for the baby because it's under water. But it's certainly more traumatic for the other people in the pool."
—Elayne Boosler

RECENTLY I HAD A LIVELY discussion with a girlfriend about our pregnancies (twenty-plus years ago). She reminisced dreamily about the "new life that grew inside of her" and how she'll always remember how protective and maternal she felt while she and her hubs, who constantly assured her she never looked more beautiful, would sit for hours rubbing her swollen belly and cooing baby talk to the unborn but obviously most amazing child ever created.

My pregnancy sucked. I gained roughly the body weight of an entire sixth grader, I had teenage acne at thirty-three, everything but brownies made me puke, and I waddled like an overstuffed Christmas goose. I did not "glow," and Hubs never once told me I looked beautiful (which was fair, because I was pregnant, not stupid, and I would've known he was lying, instantly vaporizing his future credibility about how I looked at any given moment.)

Suffice it to say that my fantasy of pregnancy didn't pass The Reality Test. Which got me to wondering how many things are better left to our imaginations. The "Great Ideas" that don't always play out *exactly* the way we pictured it in our heads.

Here are my Top 10:

1. Big dogs. Big dogs have power, presence, and through-the-roof cool factor. Big dogs also shed the equivalent of a small goat every twenty-four hours and love to sleep in the people bed, banishing humans to the outer edges of the mattress and forcing them to inhale dog hair with every breath. Big dog poops are the size of small cats and can cause nasty, prolonged neighbor wars if Fido decides the grass is greener across the fence. Unsupervised, they'll polish off the entire Christmas ham while you're pouring the wine, and the vet bills could send your firstborn to Yale for a year.

2. Stilettos. Mutually agreed by both sexes to make the female leg look longer and sexier. For the uninitiated, they can also cause awkward gaits, embarrassing faceplants, painful ankle sprains, and cranky, scary facial expressions because it's supremely painful to shove the widest part of your foot and all five toes into a tiny, pointy tip, while simultaneously putting all your weight on the balls of your feet, since your heels are jacked up too high to be of any assistance when you're trying to walk.

3. Being broke and in love. I heard a couple sigh and wistfully remember "the good old days" when they were first married and ate cold pizza every night while sitting on the floor because they were so broke, and wasn't it *wonderful*? Horse hooey. Being broke is neither romantic nor fun. Ask any broke person. It sucks. Missing the intensity and wonder of new love? Understandable. Missing not being able to pay your bills? Yeah, no.

4. Jogging. Whenever I see sneaker ads for fabulously fit women jogging down a gorgeous, tree-lined path, I develop a sudden urge to lace up and hit the pavement. Then I remember that *she* is a twenty-two-year-old supermodel, with all her body parts firmly in place, while I'm a fifty-eight-year-old grandmother, whose jogging reality includes underarms flapping like undies on a clothes line, ass bouncing like my boobs used to before gravity made them flying beagle ears, and thighs counting my steps by slamming together with each stride. No. Just no.

5. Expensive new cars. It's beautiful, it smells good, the seats are heated, and the dashboard lights up like a 747. And it's only $450 a month. You could do it. But in six months, the back seat will be the world's largest Lego box with enough spilled Goldfish to feed your kids for two days; your Great Dane will have chosen the passenger seat to hawk up the family gerbil; and the trunk will be a laundry basket for muddy soccer uniforms for kids you don't even know. And you'll still be paying $450 a month.

6. FSBO. "For Sale by Owner." How hard can it be? Why pay a realtor $30,000 to just walk some strangers through your master bedroom? Stick a sign out in the yard and sell it yourself. Yes, this has worked for some people. *We* got a steady stream of lookie-loos ("Oh, I've always wanted to see the inside of this house!" Now you have. Get out); unqualified buyers ("Gee, we've always wanted a house like this, but we can't afford it yet." Then why are you here?); and entire families (*with* dogs and kids) with ridiculous offers that could only presume we must be in foreclosure (we weren't).

7. Camping. Tried it. Hated it. Strap two days' worth of gear onto your back, hike into the woods, ignore the bugs while trying to avoid the poison oak, sleep on the ground, eat dinner off a stick, and bathe in freezing-cold water. I know our ancestors used to do this all the time. Then they invented hotels.

8. Sex every night. Great when you're young, newly in love, and living on adrenaline. Years later, sleep becomes a more precious commodity than sex. Occasional, but still great, sex keeps the marriage tingling, but "Get off me" (uttered by either party) quickly assures the required eight hours of sleep that will get us through the next work day.

9. Total honesty. I'm not advocating *lying*. But as we get older, we learn that total, unqualified honesty can tank a relationship faster than you can say, "Yes, in fact, I *am* attracted to your best friend." If I ask, "Do you like my new haircut?" (knowing I can't glue it back on if you say "Not particularly"), a simple "Yes" is appropriate. And the timeless classic, "Do these jeans make my butt look fat?" is *always* answered with, "That's not possible." Sometimes you just need to tell me what I want to hear.

10. Winning the lottery. We've all thought about it. And maybe winning a cool million would be fabulous. But who the hell needs $420 million? Your life would *never* be your own, and anyone you don't share it with now hates you. Except the tax man. He loves you. *Forever*. There's got to be a better way.

Some fantasies are great realities. Others become epic fails, but make great stories around the dinner table for our kids. In the meantime, do these jeans make my butt look big?

CHAPTER 21
Love Lessons From My Third Marriage

"To keep your marriage brimming with love, whenever you're wrong, admit it; whenever you're right, shut up."
—Ogden Nash

OKAY, I CONFESS. I'm on my third marriage.

I usually only admit to two, because my first marriage was a short-lived, youthful mismatch. We parted ways a few months after the "I do's," and we've never crossed paths again. My second marriage lasted for sixteen years but ended when we grew too far apart to find our way back as a couple. Hubs and I have been together for fifteen years and plan to pass away together, holding hands in our old age. But the statistics are not on our side.

Studies report that fifty percent of marriages in the U.S. end in divorce. That number actually increases with each successive marriage, with third marriages coming in at a seventy-three-percent failure rate. Ouch. Fortunately, I came out of my two previous marriages only slightly scathed and a little bit wiser, determined to learn how to go the distance.

Here is my Third-marriage "God Save Me from the Hell of Divorce" Lesson Plan:

1. It isn't always your turn. If your bucket list includes a stint as a circus clown, by all means, use the joint savings account to go to clown school at night while Hubs makes dinner and bathes the kids. But next year, when he announces he's joined a ridiculously expensive "Golf Lessons Around the World" club, just smile and cut the check.

2. Leave a little mystery. He loves your soft, smooth skin. He doesn't need to know that it requires a strict regimen of daily exfoliation, twice-weekly shaving, monthly bikini waxing, and an array of tweezers to snag those unexpected hairs that sprout up on your chin with mortifying regularity.

3. Sometimes it's better just to shut up. Not every subject or feeling needs to be verbally explored and analyzed like a Petri dish in chem class. That's why God invented girlfriends.

4. Avoid comparing your marriage *with friends, movie or TV couples, or country ballads.* Friends don't always tell you *everything* about their marriages. Movie couples, who spend inordinate amounts of time having uninhibited, marathon sex, are *actors*. And that country crooner who belts out a #1 heartbreak song about lost soul mates has been divorced more often than every cougar in your four kids's PTA groups combined.

5. Pick your battles. Is it really that important that he stop using the decorative couch pillows as a headrest? Yes, they'll eventually need cleaning. So clean them. Or replace them. But it's just a pillow. Let it go.

6. You can be right, or you can get laid. Good to remember when stubborn tempers begin to flare.

7. Brag about him. Like you used to when you were dating. You were charmingly annoying, constantly reminding girlfriends how gorgeous, smart, funny, and fabulous he was, how lucky you were, and didn't they all wish they could be you? Now it's, "He's an idiot, and if he thinks we're going camping, he's a *crazy* idiot."

8. Keep each other's secrets. When you live with someone for years, there are going to be personal things about him that the general public doesn't know. He slept with his piano teacher when he was seventeen. If he sees a spider, he screams like a girl until you kill it. He always wanted to be a rock star but has no actual talent, so now he air guitars it in the shower every morning. You give up the right to share this information with anyone outside the marriage, *ever*, by the law of ethics and sportsmanship.

9. Sometimes going to bed angry is the better choice. If things have reached the point where, "If he says One. More. Word. I'm going to put him *down*," it's often more judicious to part company and get some sleep, rather than pushing forward until one of you blurts out something in an exhausted, alcohol-fueled moment that can't be taken back.

10. Don't stop having fun. What did you do together before? Before the kids, the mortgage, the bills, the IRAs, and the aging parents. Do that again. Or find something new. All work and no play make both of you *boring*.

11. You can't change your partner. What you married is what you get. If there's something fundamentally "wrong" with him, stall on those wedding invitations until you figure out if you can live with it for the rest of your life.

12. Be yourself. If you have Pop-Tarts in your glovebox, or if you hate exercise, *tell him*. Many marriages tank because we try too hard to be "flawless," until we eventually collapse into an exhausted heap, face-planted into the candy bowl we keep stashed in a drawer under our workout gear, until finally confessing that the root of our weight-loss struggles is not, in fact, an inherited thyroid condition.

13. Some days, you won't be "in love." Some days, even his breathing will just *piss you off*. And some days, he'll feel the same way about *you*. We're not in high school anymore, all doe-y eyed and breathless every single day. As long as neither of you does anything stupid during this time, these moments will pass.

14. An affair has never fixed a troubled marriage. It's like borrowing money to get out of debt. It's stupid and rarely ends the way you imagined it. If your marriage is struggling, bringing Bubba the bartender into the bedroom virtually guarantees its immediate demise. Don't even think about it.

15. Marriage is not a 50/50 deal. "I'll give half and you'll give half, and that will be fair." This works if your kids are splitting the last Oreo. But in a marriage, some issues don't have an obvious halfway marker. This causes many couples to become obsessed with determining what *exactly* their half includes on any given subject. Each party needs to give 51%. Their half and *just a little bit more*. That "little bit more" is what separates the Kardashians from the Newman/Woodwards.

And there you have it. I'll look for your fiftieth anniversary party invitation in the mail.

CHAPTER 22

I Tried to be a Natural Beauty. Once. In 1974

"Beauty is the first present nature gives to women, and the first it takes away."
—Fay Weldon

OKAY, I CONFESS. I've always been a bit jealous of women who can live without beauty products. Nature babies who can hit the open road on the back of a motorcycle with all their multipurpose (shampoo, body wash, deodorant, *and* laundry detergent in one bottle) personal care items stuffed into a saddlebag, with room for clothes, headed off on a two-week trip. These women can go from bed to their inevitable a.m. yoga class in fifteen minutes flat and somehow manage to look *great*.

My morning routines are a bit more, well… complicated. I'm a product junkie, with a bathroom that friends have been known to raid instead of driving an hour to Nordstrom. There are products that cleanse, exfoliate, lift, moisturize, tone, tighten, soften, smooth (and nary a one that achieves more than one objective, hence the need for multiple products), and otherwise make you younger, sexier, thinner, and able to achieve world peace.

Do they all *work*? Yeah, no. But the guys that invented hope-in-a-jar are really, really good at what they do. If their high-gloss, full-color, wildly expensive ad in *More* magazine says that cream will erase the ever-creeping-south lines around my eyes, what the hell? I'm in. Yes, I know half these products won't deliver, but they're yummy, they smell great, and I love "the process." It makes me feel *female*. Having said that, there are days when I wish I could be more granola, less Gabor sister, and just *get going* in the morning, believing that a Colgate smile was sufficient to get out the door with confidence.

So last weekend, Hubs and I decided to spend the day cruising the valley: enjoying the hot weather in my little convertible, maybe stop for an outdoor lunch somewhere, and ultimately hitting a local winery later in the afternoon for a leisurely glass of Cabernet in the sunshine. Perfect.

I got up an hour before him and began my process. In the shower to shampoo and condition my hair (bleached within an inch of its life once every two weeks, conditioner keeps it attached to my head), then exfoliate every square inch of my body with a glove, sending unsuspecting dead skin cells screaming for their lives, and finally ending the shower with an all-over shower lotion in my favorite Chanel fragrance (leaves the bathroom smelling like an expensive French hoo-hoo house for hours afterwards, but it's *fabulous*).

Out of the shower to apply matching hoo-hoo-house body lotion over entire body, followed by a layer of no-it's-never-worked-but-hope-never-dies cellulite cream on my thighs and light cuticle oil on toes to freshen last week's pedicure. Then a drop or two of argan oil and some mousse to get my hair UP off my scalp. (It's baby fine, so without mousse, I look like a hairless cat).

The blow dryer is Hubs's signal to wake up. He stretches and yawns loudly then stumbles out of bed, takes a quick shower, brushes his teeth, runs wet hands through his hair, then tosses on jeans and a T-shirt before standing in my bathroom doorway asking, "So you ready yet?" (A question then repeated at two-minute intervals for the next thirty minutes. Yeah, *that* speeds me up).

On to the face. Apply Retin-A to reduce years of sun damage, followed by never-miss-a-day-ever 30 SPF, so there's some hope of not looking like a worn Frye boot when I'm sixty, and a collagen cream to plump up those fat little skin cells and diffuse (albeit temporarily) midlife lines. A pea-size rub of décolleté cream (I have no idea what this is for, but it's French, so it must work) and lastly, a quick swipe of lash serum to help grow the lashes that insist on falling out every time I get stressed, leaving me regularly looking like a startled wombat, and we're done. Spritz on a little fragrance, grab a pair of yoga pants (C'mon, it's the weekend) and a T-shirt, and I'm ready!

As I grab my purse, Hubs looks at me and says, "Oh, you're not wearing makeup? I can wait if you want."

Sigh. Back to the bathroom. I bet the nature babies drink all the good wine before we even get out the door.

CHAPTER 23

My Closet Has a Fabulous Life.
It's Just Not Mine

"I like my money right where I can see it… Hanging in my closet.
—Carrie Bradshaw

HUBS HAS AN UNWAVERING philosophy about my handbag. He doesn't go in there. Ever. He'll stand right next to my purse and announce "I need the checkbook," and no amount of cajoling, stated permission, or exasperated replies on my part to "just get in there and get it" will persuade him to stick his hand in there.

He feels the same way about my closet.

Women's closets, he informs me, are *personal,* with everything organized "just so," the way a woman wants it, and a man would have to be fundamentally insane to go in there and start handling stuff or moving it around.

So last weekend, when I asked him to add an additional shelf inside my closet, he replied, "Only if you move your clothes out of the way. And all your shoes." I tried every argument I could think of to convince him that this task was unnecessary, but he wasn't budging.

Fine. Out it all came. As I laid an entire walk-in closetful of clothes across the king-size bed, I learned that while women's *closets* are forbidden territory, the *bed* is everybody's game.

Hubs began to pick through the stacks, holding up item after item, saying, "I like this. Why don't you wear this?" over and over again, until it began to feel like a Hindu mantra, and he started to wonder why he's believed for years that all I owned was one pair of black slacks and three pairs of yoga pants. I couldn't tell him that my closet was living a life I no longer had. It appeared to be time for some serious revamping.

With my new shelf installed and Hubs shooed out the door for a blissful afternoon of uninterrupted televised sports, I began to sort, vowing to eliminate anything that no longer fit my body, my life, or (ouch) my age. Buh-bye to the following:

1. Anything that doesn't fit. I'm talking about the body I have right now, today. Not the body I'm going to have after I lose the same ten pounds I've been working on since 1989. Not the body I'm going to have once I start working out again, someday. This body, right now.

2. Stilettos. Red patent, four-and-a-half-inch heels, pointed toe. Hubs immediately zeroed in on those with a big grin when he spied them underneath a sweater pile. But who am I kidding? I have Parkinson's. I've fallen off my Reeboks. I finally decided to just toss them in Hubs's closet for trips down memory lane.

3. Anything that looks better on my DIL than on me. If I'm unsure about something in my closet, I have my twenty-six-year-old daughter-in-law try it on. Then I try it on me. If it's obvious to my six-year-old grandson that it looks better on Mommy than on Grandma and was clearly designed for a body whose breasts are still up near her clavicles *and* whose butt is not yet showing the effects of gravity or an expired gym membership, DIL gets to take it home.

4. Cowboy boots. Filed in the "What the hell was I thinking?" section of my closet. I don't live on a ranch, ride horses, or farm. Kind of like walking down the street in a wetsuit when you've never been in the water.

5. One-piece Miracle swimsuit, "guaranteed to make you look ten pounds thinner." Miracle, my ass. When you stuff a size-eight body into a size-six piece of flesh-crushing Lycra, you get the swimsuit version of muffin top, with fat squishing out like errant toothpaste over the top and under the butt cheeks. Lesson learned. No item of clothing can make fat disappear like a Las Vegas bar trick. Cramming it into one area is just going to shove it out somewhere else.

6. Trendy jeans for a body I don't have. Low-rise jeans on a woman with a long waist guarantees a porno peek down your backside every time you bend over or squat down, and since the world does not need to see another fifty-seven-year-old butt crack,

I'm retiring these. Ditto for my beloved boyfriend jeans, with the comfy, slouchy fit, that caused Hubs to remark, "I'm surprised that a woman who cares as much about how she looks as you do would wear those jeans." *Boom*. And gone.

7. Palazzo-style jumpsuit. Recently purchased, surprisingly flattering, and stupidly expensive, but never worn because it makes me feel like a bleached Donna Summer, looking for a disco ball and a karaoke machine for a slightly drunken wailing of "Last Dance." The problem with living through a trend the first time is that it feels "costumey" the second time.

8. Spandex dress. Super-hot when Hubs and I were first together, I was fifteen pounds thinner, and we were… well, *dating*. Dinner, dancing, foreplay. All that dating entails when you're falling in love and the other person's breathing fascinates you. Now a blissful day together is spent working on the house or cleaning up the yard, and nothing screams "I'm trying to look younger, but now I just look ridiculous" than a middle-aged woman topping her arborvitaes in a spandex dress.

9. Faux accessories. I'm talking mostly handbags here. Knockoffs may suit the budget and fashion needs of the twenty-something set, but by the time you're fifty-plus, they seem a bit like we're trying too hard to pretend to be something we're not. I buy the best I can afford and leave the pretend labels to the young.

10. Maxi dresses. I have two. I've never worn either one. By this age, we pretty much know what our best features are and what body parts we should be flashing. Maxi dresses look best on tall, willowy-thin women with toned arms. I'm five foot three and curvy; my legs are my best feature, but my arms could use a few weeks with a Shake Weight. Maxi dresses hide my legs and show off my jiggly guns, and, unless I'm in four-inch platforms (see #2), make me look like an Amish hobbit.

So now my closet is beautifully organized, with two pairs of black slacks and three pairs of yoga pants. Nordstrom is having a sale. I'm going in.

CHAPTER 24

9 Ways to Light Up Your Man (or Not)

"Women need a reason to have sex. Men just need a place."
—Billy Crystal

I WAS RECENTLY RUNNING a Google search for material on another post, and up popped a dropdown selection of ways to spice things up in ye' ole marital bedroom.

Congenitally incapable of not going where I shouldn't, I clicked on a few links. Three hours later, my cheeks hurt from laughing out loud at the visuals in my head, as I imagined Hubs's responses, and I'd completely forgotten what I'd originally sat down to research. But whatever it was, this was *way* better.

I decided to share some of the best suggestions with you because, well, that's the generous kind of person I am. Who knows? Maybe I can save a marriage or two. What can't be resolved by a teenage-style make-out session in the family SUV? You're welcome.

1. Send him on a "Love Hunt." Similar to a treasure hunt, but he must drive all over town, asking storeowners if they're hiding something for him from his wife. Suggestions were the liquor store for his favorite beverage; the florist for their limited-edition "You're My Hot Stuff" bouquet; and Safeway for a half-dozen "I Heart my Husband" balloons.

Yeah, no.

Hubs *hates* to run errands, and although I could probably sell him on the liquor store, I'm reasonably certain, after fifteen years together, that flowers and balloons wouldn't get him where I wanted him to go.

2. Sex up the bathtub. Light a couple dozen candles, draw a deep bubble bath, and pour the champagne. Get into the tub and call him with, "Babe, can you bring me a towel?" The theory is that he'll take one look at you lounging naked and bubbly in the tub, backlit by the soft glow of the candlelight, and be diving in to join you before the water cools.

The one time I tried something similar (two candles, wine, and no bubbles), Hubs dashed down the hall with a towel and tossed it through the open bathroom door with nary a glance, yelling "Gonzaga is up by *twelve!*" as he ran back to the living room to watch the game.

3. Take personal photos of your man so everyone can see what a stud he is. Suggestions included cowboy hat and boots, pajamas, briefs or boxers, and of course, "nekkid,"

Just… Wow.

My brain just can't formulate an appropriate way to ask Hubs if I can photograph him in his birthday suit, wearing nothing but a cowboy hat and boots, so all my Facebook friends can see what a hunka-hunk I married.

4. Kidnap him. Walk in, unannounced, to his workplace, and hold a toy gun on him while you handcuff his wrists and take him away for "secret interrogation."

Oh. My. God.

Any visual of me walking onto Hubs' job site and slapping handcuffs on him then carting him away for an obvious afternoon of motel-room boogie ends with him being totally mortified, while the scene is embellished and replayed for weeks at every construction site in town. I'm not sure that making your man the laughingstock of his industry for the next year is the way to his… well, you know.

5. Share his favorite sport by initiating sex with him on the football field, the soccer field, or in the gym. Because nothing turns a man on like having his name in the local paper for public nudity and indecency after getting caught having sex in a public stadium by the high school marching band. All forty-two members.

6. Give him you as a present. Cover yourself with sticky bows and let him take them off one by one.

Before we get started, who puts the bows on any area I can't reach? I scrolled my speed-dial list and couldn't find a single person I'd be comfortable calling to ask if they would come over and slap red bows on my naked behind. As for Hubs peeling them off? Possibly the world's worst Brazilian.

7. Send him to work with a balloon bouquet. Fill his car with balloons that have tiny "I love you" notes inside, and leave a pin with a note that says he has to pop all the balloons before he can get into his car.

Maybe I'm getting old, but this would just piss me off. Trying to get out the door to work and finding my car full of cutesy teenage-appropriate balloons that I had to pop and then clean up before I went to work would *not* be foreplay.

8. Take a walk in the rain, wearing nothing but your raincoat and rain boots.

Are you *high*?

Walking in the rain is one of those things that sounds more romantic than it really is. And the mental image of me, standing in the rain, shivering, with hair plastered to my head and water running down my face, flashing Hubs in nothing but rubber boots and fifty-eight-year-old boobs would pretty much guarantee never getting laid again.

9. Be Jane and Tarzan. Him in a loincloth and you in a leopard print bikini. Feed him by hand from a bowl of nuts, fruits, and berries while jungle drums play on your iPod.

Few things leave me speechless.

This *might* have worked in my twenties. But Midlife Jane, still trying to work the leopard thong, with body parts having migrated visibly southward and butt jiggling in time to the jungle drums as I snuggle up to Hubs with a handful of berries, is more likely to send him screaming for an eye wash station.

At this point, I decided that the best way to find out what would fire Hubs up would be to *ask him*. "That's easy," he grinned. "Greet me at the door. Naked. Holding a beer and a sandwich."

Notwithstanding the fact that, at fifty-eight, naked is not my best presentation, I can do that. What the hell. As long as it doesn't involve balloons.

CHAPTER 25

Living the Frugal Life. Not So Much

"The best things in life are free. The second-best are very expensive."
— Coco Chanel

ONE RECENT, SUNNY AFTERNOON, I decided to make a quick stop at the Taco Bell drive-through, and, feeling pleased with my sudden surge of frugality, I reminded the clerk that I was eligible for the senior discount. He replied that although they didn't actually have a discount, they did offer "older people" a free soft drink. Resisting the urge to kill my good mood by reaching through the window and smacking the insolent pup on the back of his head, I smiled and agreed to take the deal.

My 1974 car was built before cup holders, so I set my drink carefully on the console and began to pull forward, forgetting that my car has a tendency to surge at will when you press the gas pedal. Unfortunately, it willed and immediately lunged forward, just hard enough to toss my drink in one direction and the lid in another, spraying the entire interior of my car, including the dashboard, windshield, and sheepskin covers, with sticky, icy cola. *Seriously*?

A quick calculation told me I did save $1.20 on the Diet Coke, but it cost me $100 to clean the inside of my car. This frugal thing may not be for me.

Generally speaking, when I hear the word "frugal," my brain conjures up visions of living in a yurt, weaving my own clothes, and wearing Birkenstocks year-round. Frugal living seems to bear more than a passing resemblance to dieting. Its entire premise is based on *deprivation*. "Here, take this notepad and write down everything to like to eat/buy. That's going to be your list of things *you can never have again*." Awesome.

But it's hard to argue with the fact that today's economy often requires cutting back on non-necessities. Like many couples, Hubs and I have spent countless evenings ferreting out exactly where the money went that month and whether or not we can avoid or reduce that expense next month. Like DEA dogs sniffing out cocaine at LAX, we're constantly on the hunt for hidden spending habits that need to be eliminated.

Then, a few weeks ago, I received a newsletter from a local financial guru, promoting his upcoming talk on "How to Live a Frugal but Fabulous Life," and it included these "fun tips" on saving money:

1. Buy generic brands. This only works if the generic brand is actually edible. Some are fine. Others are just plain nasty. Hint: If it comes in a large plastic bag and the leprechaun on the front looks more like a garden gnome, it doesn't taste like Lucky Charms.

2. Buy in bulk. Unless you have four refrigerators and eat a *lot* of hamburgers, who the hell needs twelve bottles of ketchup? And "Split it between friends" assumes someone (yeah, that would be *you*) is supposed to drive all over town to deliver the other eleven bottles and collect the money. I've already got two jobs.

3. Reuse your paper towels. So now I've either got a clothes line in my kitchen, or every surface is constantly covered with drying paper towels that we can reuse later that day. If you're OCD, this will make your head explode.

4. Wait until the washing machine and dishwasher are full before you run them. Since there's only two of us, that means I'll be standing in the kitchen tomorrow morning, buck naked, with a dirty fry pan.

5. Take your cans in and recycle them yourself. By the time I repeatedly stuck 100 cans in those constantly-jamming recycle machines at the local supermarket, I was pissed off and covered with sticky cola residue. The $3 I made didn't cover the ninety-minute relaxation massage and cleaning costs required to regain my Zen.

6. Clip coupons. Perfect. Now I get to become one of those women who backs up a line at Safeway for twenty-five minutes while she digs for the appropriate coupon in her erroneously named "EZ Coupon Finder" notebook, and then proceeds to argue with the cashier about the expiration date, until a manager has to be called over the loudspeaker to come down and resolve the issue. This is a small town. We know where you live, and we hate you.

7. Set up all your bills on Auto Pay, *to avoid late fees*. Don't. Think. So. Financial experts are constantly warning us to keep our banking information secure and confidential, but then, because it's a business request, we happily hand over our account numbers and all our personal information, which is immediately emailed to an English-as-a-ninth-language clerk in their Billing Department in Sri Lanka. Like *that's* never backfired on anyone. And once they take the money out, good luck trying to get it back.

8. Make your own housecleaning products. I tried that once. In an ill-advised attempt to create a better bathroom cleaner than what was on the market, I poured every cleaning product we had into a big bucket, including bleach and ammonia. Almost blew the house up, and it took months for my eyelashes to grow back. Moving on.

9. Ditch the gym membership and work out at home. Good idea, if you're not ADHD. Thirty minutes on the elliptical trainer takes two hours to accomplish if you're getting off every other minute to put the clothes in the dryer, let the dogs out, answer the phone, and check your blog stats. Who's got the time?

10. Take home extra sugar and condiment packages from fast-food restaurants. Because nothing says "class" like serving your family and guests dinner with bowls of ketchup packets you boosted from the local McD's.

11. Don't flush after just a pee. Wait until it matters. Wow. Few things leave me speechless.

Hubs and I have our own way of being frugal. On those days we're just itching to go on a spending bender, we head out to Costco and spend the afternoon happily going up and down every aisle, piling our cart high with every single "really cool and amazingly-low-priced" item we just can't live without. Then we park the cart at the front of the store and dash across the street to the Wooden Chicken Pub for cheap lunch and drinks, feeling the rush of shopping without spending any money.

White-trash frugality at its finest.

CHAPTER 26

Trying to Lose Weight?
12 Stupidest Weight Loss Ideas, Ever

"My heart says chocolate and wine, but my jeans say, for the love of God, woman, eat a salad."
—Unknown

RECENTLY I SAW A TELEVISION interview with a self-proclaimed money expert who said that if you want to get rich, you should start a religion or discover a new diet.

Apparently, a great majority of Americans are spiritually confused or fat. Notwithstanding the fact that we live in a culture where a size twelve makes you a "plus-size" model, while the average American woman wears a size fourteen, making our barometer for "fat" a bit skewed, many Get-Rich-Quick gurus believe that if you can address this issue with something people haven't heard before, no matter how bizarre it is, you'll be christening your new yacht before all the checks have cleared the bank.

This got me thinking about all the goofy, stupid, or just plain dangerous lengths people have gone to in our repeated but failed attempts to take off tonnage that years of crappy food choices, excess alcohol, and sloth-level exercise programs have put on. Intelligent, educated people will believe the most idiotic pitch if a product or plan promises "rapid weight loss"; if the tag line is "without the need for exercise!" we're lambs to a slaughter.

In case you've missed any, here are my favorite, actually-searchable-on-Google *Stupid Weight-Loss Ideas*.

1. Salt your food after a couple of bites. I'm talking *lots and lots* of salt. So you won't or can't eat it. I tried that once on a piece of chocolate cake but discovered two hours later that, if you scrape the salty layer off, you can still eat the rest, so that idea was just dumb.

2. Take pictures of yourself naked. From every angle. Front, back, and sides. Tape up the photos where you can see them easily whenever you're in the mood to overeat, i.e., your fridge or your bathroom mirror. Mother of God. One look at those pics and I decided to kill myself, so what difference does an entire pan of brownies make now?

3. Eat with your non-dominant hand. Yeah, tried that, too. I was at a formal fundraiser dinner party and impaled my cheek with a shrimp fork, bleeding all over the communal shrimp bowl. The hostess hasn't spoken to me since.

4. Use smaller plates to reduce your portions. Makes as much sense as drinking wine out of a shot glass so you'll drink less. This just means multiple trips back to the kitchen to refill your tiny little plate, forcing Hubs to pause the movie every time you get up. Longest version of *Titanic,* ever.

5. Eat cotton balls to trick your stomach into feeling full. It's true. Supermodels around the globe have discovered that eating cotton balls fills your stomach by expanding and taking up space (think tampons for the intestines), so you'll feel full and won't actually eat calorie-laden celery sticks. You just can't make this stuff up. My response to this one is... Nope, I've got nothin'.

6. Purposely wear your tightest clothes to remind you how fat you've become, reducing your temptation to overeat. Yeah, because beating the crap out of your self-esteem all day long works really well, until you get home and rip those damn pants off, toss them out the bedroom window, and dive headfirst into a large bowl of Doritos and Velveeta cheese dip, because you're fat, you always have been fat, you always will be fat, and you just don't care anymore.

7. Just breathe. Then don't eat. Ever. Breatharians believe that the human body can sustain itself from the sun, water, fresh air, and the Prana or life force that runs through all. Wiley Brookes, the movement's founder, says herbal teas and water are all we really need. It's hard to disclaim his statement, because his followers are mostly dead. He says that's because they "didn't do it right." Personally, I don't trust a man whose first name is "Wiley."

8. Eat baby food. (Reportedly, Reese Witherspoon is a fan of this one.) The upsides are that it's portable, easy to digest, and portion controlled. But it's also nutritionally designed for *babies*, not the average, adult-size female. The jarred meats might be passable as really-awful cracker spreads if you were really drunk, but pureed spinach will never be a smoothie. And unless you have a small child living with you, have these shipped to you online. They're harder to explain in your grocery cart than your Depends.

9. Eat with chopsticks. This worked for a short time, as my spastic chopsticks shot food everywhere but into my mouth. But determination breeds skill, so I was quickly able to eat everything from nachos to ice cream with an impressive flick of my sticks. New skill. Still fat.

10. Eat a tapeworm. *Disgusting*? Yes. Effective? Yes. It also causes bloating, diarrhea, seizures, and dementia. And they're hard to come by. You can't exactly pick one up at Rite Aid. Even supermodels won't go here. These girls eat *cotton* but think this is stupid. 'Nuf said.

11. Eat only things you can fit into a pita pocket. They're thinking cherry tomatoes, broccoli, fruit slices, and small portions of meat or poultry. Bahahahaha. My pita pockets easily carried two bite-size Snickers bars, a handful of Milk Duds, three Oreo cookies, and one large frosted brownie with walnuts. Didn't lose any weight, but found a cool way to eat dessert while standing.

12. Drink alcohol instead of eating. It burns faster than food. Millions of people are on this and don't realize it's a diet program. They're called alcoholics. If your liver (and your marriage) survives this, it comes with a free month at Serenity Lane.

And so it would seem that eating healthy foods, watching our portions, getting regular exercise, and reducing our alcohol intake is, in fact, the only way to lose weight and live to show it off.

I'm so screwed.

CHAPTER 27

I Read *Snow White* to my Granddaughter. Now I'm Paying for Her Therapy

"Life is Not a Fairy Tale. If You Lose Your Shoe at Midnight, You're Drunk."
—Unknown

MY DAUGHTER-IN-LAW RECENTLY sent me a list of items my two-year-old granddaughter might like for Christmas. Apparently she's discovered books, so the list included several traditional fairy tales.

The next day, I was at the local bookstore, leafing through some classic choices, and I suddenly realized how disturbing many of these stories might be to a small child. Seriously, these books could scare the crap out of a toddler. There are giants that eat small boys, forest animals that devour your grandma, evil stepmothers who want to kill you or lock you in an attic, and moms that abandon you in the woods to be cooked in a psycho-lady's oven.

I understand that fairy tales have been around forever, that we grew up on them and (arguably) turned out fine, and that they provide children with enthralling examples of the triumph of good over evil. So before total strangers start accusing me of hating storybooks, children, and all things related to the sanctity of motherhood, I'm not suggesting a household ban on fairy tales. I do, however, question their validity as *bedtime stories.*

At two or three years of age, as our tiny progeny drifts off to sleep, listening to how Snow White's stepmother put a contract out on her, and then, when that failed, decided to poison Snowy herself, it feels less like a tale about a handsome prince and his beautiful princess living happily ever after, and more like a child's version of *Criminal Minds*.

1. Little Red Riding Hood. A story about a little girl taking goodies to her beloved grandma, walking alone in the woods (yeah, good plan), while being stalked by a wolf that wants to eat her. Wolfie rushes to grandma's house to get there before the little girl does, where he eats the grandmother, puts on her clothes, and lies in wait for the child. When she arrives, he kills her and eats her, too. Good luck getting that kid to summer camp.

2. Hansel and Gretel. A tale about a poor, forest-dwelling family, where Mom decides to ease their financial burdens by having Dad take the two kids out into the woods and abandon them. Dad doesn't really like the idea, but he's a pussy, so he agrees. Hansel and Gretel overhear the plan, so Hansel drops white stones behind them as they travel into the forest. The kids follow the stones and return home. Mom's pissed and instructs Dad to try again. This time, the children mark their trail with bread crumbs, but the crumbs get eaten by birds, and the kids are basically screwed. Eventually, they get lucky and stumble across a house made of sugar and candy, only to discover it's owned by an old woman who plans to bake the kids in her furnace and eat them. She locks Hansel in a cage until Gretel ultimately shoves the old bat into the fire where she burns to death. Wow. If you ever take your children hiking in the forest after this story, don't be surprised to find them a little clingy.

3. Jack and the Beanstalk. Jack and his family were poor and starving. So Jack plants some beans for food, and they grow into a large beanstalk. Jack shimmies up the beanstalk and discovers that it leads to a huge castle belonging to an evil giant. The giant wants to eat Jack by grinding him into his bread. While in the castle, Jack discovers a goose that lays golden eggs. He steals the goose so he and his mother can live a life of leisure. On the next trip up, Jack discovers a golden harp. When he steals that, too, the giant tries to run down the beanstalk to get it back, but Jack chops the beanstalk down and the giant falls to his death. Jack and his mother live happily ever after on the giant's gold. The moral? Steal it, and kill the owner when he tries to get it back.

4. Snow White and the Seven Dwarfs. A young girl gets an evil stepmother who is so jealous of her that she instructs a hunter to take her out and kill her. He won't do it, so Stepmom decides to do it herself by giving Snowy a poisoned apple. Snowy runs away from home and moves into a house with seven men she doesn't know. Eventually, a handsome prince saves her with a kiss. The stereotypes in here are rampant (Stepmom is evil; girl is saved by boy), and Snow White's decision to run away and live with a houseful of men she knows nothing about could have ended differently, not to mention is a stupid message to send to a little girl.

5. Cinderella. Again with the evil stepmother cliché, but this time with two equally-nasty stepsisters. They're all so jealous of Cindy that they make her a scullery maid and otherwise keep her locked in the attic with the mice. She never figures out a way to help herself, and years go by, until one day she gets a fairy godmother and a prince, who step in and magically change her life. Do we really want to teach our daughters to be helpless victims until a fairy godmother and a rich man suddenly materialize to solve their problems? One doesn't exist, and the other makes up one percent of the population. I'd rather teach my granddaughter how to kick bully ass on her way out the door.

And so I put down the beautifully illustrated, but oddly dark, boxed set of *Classic Fairy Tales* and picked up the entire series of *Winnie the Pooh and the Hundred-Acre Woods*. I love that donkey. And I'm just not ready to explain those dwarfs.

CHAPTER 28

When is "Bite Me" an Appropriate Response to a Compliment?

"I hate it when you offer someone a sincere compliment on their mustache, and suddenly she's not speaking to you anymore."
—Unknown

MUCH HAS BEEN WRITTEN over the years on how to graciously accept a compliment. We teach our daughters to simply say "Thank you," instead of automatically becoming self-deprecating ("This old thing? I've had it for years.") or coy ("Do you really?") when someone says, "I love your dress." Personally, I'm still waiting for the day when it's okay to reply, "You're right. I look *hot* in this dress." But God forbid we should appear vain or conceited, so we smile and voice some oversight ("I didn't have time for makeup"), suggesting we left the house that morning hoping, but appropriately uncertain, that we looked suitable for public viewing.

Over the years (fifty-eight, if you're counting), I've concluded that many of us are marginally skilled at *receiving* compliments but woefully abysmal at *giving* them. We pepper our compliments with qualifiers (*"for your age"*) or wide-eyed, pseudo-innocence ("Gee, I could *never* do what you're doing."). The kind of statements that you're taught to respond to with "Thank you," while your brain is silently replying, "Bite me."

Assuming you're not a total male douche and still think "You know what would look good on you, baby? Me" is an acceptable compliment to any female, of any age, *ever*, or you're a woman who thinks another woman, barely half-dozen years older than you, loves to be told she "looks exactly like her mother" (in which case you're both so lost, I can't help you), I'm offering up the ten worst compliments I've ever personally received, in hopes of providing a glimpse into what we're *really* thinking when we say "Thank you."

1. "You look fabulous for your age." What does that *mean*? I look great because I don't look fifty-eight? Is fifty-eight a bad thing to look like? If I told you I was forty-eight, would I still look fabulous? Or would you be thinking, "She's only *forty-eight*? *Damn*, she looks ten years older." And when was the last time you told a twenty-four-year-old that she looked fabulous for her age?

2. "Not many women your age can wear their hair that short." There's that pesky qualifier again: "your age." *Stop that.* So now I'm left wondering if you're really saying I resemble a hairless cat and should grow my hair, starting *today*. This is the stepsister compliment to "My husband would never let me cut my hair that short." What is this, *1956*? Who says, "My husband wouldn't *let me...*" anymore? I just smile and reply, "Yes, thankfully my hubs has a thing for human Chihuahuas."

3. *(After telling a co-worker I was starting a new diet)* **"You don't need to diet. Your husband likes voluptuous women. *My* hubs likes thin women. But you're lucky because you don't have to worry about it."** Ouch. There's so much wrong with this one, I hardly know where to start. Since you not-so-subtly stated that I'm fortunate because my husband prefers fat women, we're just going to end our Facebook friendship right now, before this escalates into a public, online brawl, *WITH CAPS.*

4. "You're fifty-eight? Congratulations." Huh? Turning fifty-eight is not an achievement or something we get some kind of middle-age trophy for. It just happens. All by itself. Seriously, I never put it on my Life Goals storyboard, so no congratulations are necessary. If you wouldn't say it to a thirty-year-old, don't say it to a fifty-year-old.

5. "Of course you can still wear a bikini. You've earned it. You deserve to flaunt whatever body you've got." Whatever body I've got? Swell. Now I'm not going to the beach unless I'm wearing a burka. In black. At night.

6. "Older women look better a little heavier." While this may be true, I've yet to meet *any* woman who likes to be referred to as either "older" or "heavier," particularly in the same sentence. A double-don't. (And for the love of God, never substitute "mature" for "older." You're likely to be shoved out of the car. While it's moving.)

7. "I love your white hair. But aren't you afraid it makes you look older?" No, actually, because that's what I was going for. Fifty-eight seemed so, well… young, so I was going for seventy. But thank you for letting me know it's working.

8. "You look great. Where do you get your work done?" Say *what*? This is the equivalent of "When are you due?" to a woman who is *not pregnant*. The latter suggests she's either packing around an extra human or she's simply fat, and the former suggests she couldn't possibly look that good without a little surgical intervention. Either way, you better hope she's not your Secret Santa at next year's office Christmas party.

9. "Great dress. I admire you for still going sleeveless." That's okay. It's a public service. When I raise my arms, the local meteorologist can tell the wind direction and speed by the flapping of my underarms like windsocks on a barn. You're welcome. Now excuse me while I go get a sweater.

10. (*By a saleswoman.*) **"You'd look great in this dress. And we have a full selection of Spanx on the second floor."** Gee thanks, but since what you're saying is that I'd have to stuff myself into a spandex toothpaste tube to wear the dress, I think I'll pass.

So ladies, if we meet on the street, let's just say "You look *fabulous*, dahling," "Oh, so do *you*," and leave it at that. And men, if you're compelled to comment on a woman's looks, a simple "You're pretty" (or some similar variation thereof, *without* a qualifier like "for your age") will be less likely to result in her feeling compared to your mother and/or accidentally (oops) spilling her drink in your lap.

Until we meet again. Did I mention you look *hot* in that dress?

·

CHAPTER 29
Rules of Engagement. How to Keep the Love Alive

"I love you no matter what you do, but do you have to do so much of it?"
—Jean Illsley Clarke

·

THERE'S A MOMENT IN EVERY marriage when the relationship shifts from Phase I, where everything your partner says is oh-so-witty and even his *breathing* fascinates you, to Phase II, where the love, although deeper and fuller, feels a little less "hot."

Maybe it happened overnight after a single, unfortunate event (the night he got drunk at your office Christmas party and told everyone you've been wearing Depends for the last three years) or gradually, from years of tiny irritations (*must* he clip his toenails at the dining table?) that have built up into a lengthy list of Things You Do That Piss Me Off.

But Phase I, while exhilarating and exciting, is not practical over the long haul. Fueled by twenty-four-hour-a-day endorphins (often accompanied by copious amounts of alcohol), Phase I is suspended reality. Long nights of endless gazing at each other like besotted teenagers who've recently discovered sex eventually gives way to jobs, bills, kids, friends, and family obligations. A too-lengthy Phase I would inevitably find us living in our cars, unemployed, and on the wait-list for Serenity Lane.

But with the passing of Phase I, even though the love remains, sometimes less-glowing feelings can begin to emerge. Previously cute quirks now start to become annoying. That joke he tells at *every single party* isn't as funny anymore. His once-comforting snoring now sounds like a bullhorn, and you haven't had a good night's sleep in weeks. And if he doesn't stop drinking the milk directly out of the damn carton, you're going to knock out a wall and install your own refrigerator. "'Til death do us part" is beginning to feel like a long ways away.

Fortunately, there are things we can do to remember how we ended up married in the first place. Assuming this union wasn't prearranged by your elders, a marriage of convenience, or simply a business merger, experts offer a few tips to help keep the passion alive.

1. Once a week or so, spend one evening together without discussing whose purchase overdrew the checking account, how long your mother intends to stay when she comes out next spring, or whether or not it's time for Johnny Junior to start posting his own bail. Movies, travel, books, hobbies. Dating stuff. FYI, this is harder than it sounds.

2. If you fight, try to keep it from escalating into an all-out street brawl, where things get blurted out that can't be unsaid. "Yes, I did sleep with your best friend, but it was only because you were going through that freaky male-menopause thing, and you couldn't get it up" is not helpful if you were originally arguing over why he didn't take the dog to the groomers.

3. Pick your battles. It's not necessary to point out every single thing he does that annoys you, every single time. ("*Must* you leave your wet towel on the floor *every. friggin'. day*?" "*Seriously*? You forgot to get bread *again*?") Little bitches, if repeated often enough, can make you seem like a big one.

4. Ask for what you want. It's been scientifically established that men don't get "hints," no matter how obvious we think we're being. ("I dragged you past that necklace in the window *eight times*, and you bought me a blender?") It's the same for household chores. Want him to fold that pile of laundry you dumped right next to him on the couch? Ask. Preferably without sarcasm or eye-rolling.

5. If you forgive, forget. Forgiveness of another's transgressions doesn't mean, "I'll let you off the hook for drunk-flirting with the hot new neighbor at the Fourth of July block party, but I reserve the right to revisit this grievance whenever I'm pissed off or hurt by another stupid thing you did." This is not "forgiving." It's stockpiling another grenade in your marital Waco arsenal to be used whenever you want to really nail his ass.

6. Every once in a while, be the woman he fell in love with. The one who adored him, who laughed at all of his jokes and bragged about him to her girlfriends. Many of us can instantly verbalize our partner's top-twenty faults but are inexplicably tongue-tied when asked to come up with his five best qualities. Ouch.

7. Stop trying to change or improve him. When we get married, we profess to love someone "just the way they are," but then launch a Def-Con 10 makeover the day after we say "I do." He needs to quit smoking, join a gym, sell his Harley, and stop wearing those ridiculous fraternity T-shirts. Maybe so. But imagine *your* reaction if he rolled over the morning after the wedding and said, "You know, babe, it'd sure be great if you could knock off a few pounds."

8. Strike while the iron's hot. Too often, with so many other tasks clamoring for another chunk of our day, we wait for "the perfect moment" to have sex, to connect and be together. Perfection is not only overrated, it's *rare*. If the mood hits you and you two aren't alone? Stuff the dogs in the bathroom, send any offspring with a driver's license to the store, and plop the wee ones in front of the big-screen TV for the 300th viewing of *Frozen*. They'll still go to college someday. Spontaneous play is important for big people, too.

One evening, as Hubs and I were driving home from a restaurant, I commented (okay, whined) that he didn't seem to be paying much attention to me lately. As we pulled into the driveway and got out of the car, Hubs' Chihuahua, Chi Chi, tore out of the house, yapping and twirling, tail wagging and body shaking with uninhibited, eager delight to see him until finally she air-Jordaned over the porch into his arms, proceeding to enthusiastically lick his face like he'd been gone for months instead of hours.

Hubs looked over at me and grinned, "When you start greeting me at the door like this, I promise you'll have my full attention."

Ten-pound dog. 120-pound human missile. It won't be quite the same, but I'm willing to give it a try.

CHAPTER 30

I Auditioned to be a Spanx Model.
It's Been Six Months, and They Haven't Called

"Inside every older person is a younger person wondering what the hell happened."
—Cora Harvey Armstrong

IN *GONE WITH THE WIND,* they were called "corsets." Our mothers called them "girdles." Our generation knows them as "Spanx." Tiny pieces of tight spandex designed to lift, tighten, squish, shove, and compress evidence of our age, our expired gym memberships from 2007, and our post-menopausal passion for Girl Scout Thin Mints and red wine (yes, *together*).

Spanx come in a dizzying variety of options, for all body shapes and concerns. But I've concluded that Spanx work best on women who don't need them.

My Spanx catalog arrived last week, and I sat down to flip through it, happily envisioning the new me, all toned and tightened without having to sweat it up on a Tread Climber or replace my Marie Callendar's freezer stash with boxes of Jenny Craig. *Seriously,* people? Every girl in the catalog would look fabulous in dental floss and nipple pasties. They all appeared to be seventeen and six feet tall, with mile-long legs and zero-percent body fat, and had obviously never given birth or experienced the guilty pleasure of cheese fries at the county fair. Where were the 5'3", fifty-eight-year-old grandmothers, who have two jobs and can only work out at 4:00 a.m. (meaning, they don't), and who have an unfortunate desire to eat two to three times every day?

It was then that I got the Big Idea. I'd send the Spanx people a few full-length selfies in several styles, for "real advertising." My mind was whirling with visuals that could never be unseen.

In an effort to not preempt this brilliant advertising concept (it's only been six months; they could still call, right?), I'm not including the pics I sent to the Spanx team in this book. But here are some observations I noted during my walks down the runway (my hallway) wearing nothing but Spanx and a smile.

Generally speaking, the entire concept is based on stuffing a curvy size-X body into a teensy size-Y stretchy toothpaste tube. To be effective, you must break a sweat getting into it. If it slips on like granny panties, you need the next size down. And remember, the fat or loose skin you're compressing doesn't just go away. More often than not, it squishes out over the top, around the back, or below your buttocks. The part of you *under* the fabric will appear fabulously toned and tightened, but what oozes out from the top and bottom can make you look like a super-stuffed burrito.

1. The Slimmer & Shine Open Bust, Mid-Thigh Body Shaper. Basically, shorts that go from thighs to waist, with spaghetti-strap suspenders. I looked like a German yodeler in the world's ugliest Lederhosen. Includes "butt pockets" to boost the hiney up and out. While the side shoulder straps did help prevent my boobs from flopping over and becoming back fat whenever I lay down, the thigh bands resulted in unfortunate reverse muffin tops, with rippley thigh skin migrating out from the bottom of each pantie leg. And after spending the last several decades battling a big-booty gene pool, I'm inherently resistant to paying a hundred bucks for something that pads my ass.

2. Super Higher Power Shaper. A tight shaper that runs from the mid-thigh to just under the boobs. Compresses the entire general area, including thighs, waist, and rear. Again, with the butt lifter. Apparently I'm not grasping the big-butt trend, started by J. Lo and evolving into a nationwide pursuit by Kim Kardashian. While I appreciate any fashion trend that honors women who eat, whenever I think of butt pads, my mind sees spandex fanny packs. Can't do it.

3. Open Bust Camisole. Essentially just the top half of #1. Could work, but the bottom of the cami persisted in riding up towards my waist, necessitating repeated efforts to reach up and pull it back down. If the point of wearing a human Scrunchie is to look better, constantly sticking your hands up your shirt all day to readjust your underwear is not going to get you there.

4. Lingerie-Strap Slip. I tried this one under Hubs's favorite LBD on Date Night. It felt a bit like a sausage casing, but I did look smoother. All good until we got home and, feeling sparky, Hubs unzipped my dress. As it slid to the floor and I stood wearing nothing but a mortified expression in what he later described as a giant, vacuum-sealed Food Saver bag, he burst into unrestrained laughter, choking out, "What the *hell* are you wearing, woman?" Hubs slept in the guest room, and I mailed that one to my sister the next morning. Good luck with that, Sissy.

5. Lust-Have Slimming Teddy. Surprisingly sexy little bodysuit, with lace and demi-cup bra. Fun, if you're young and your boobs are non-existent or purchased and your butt is still perky. In other words, if you look good in a bikini. In daylight. After twenty minutes of struggling to get into it and get all my body parts properly stuffed into position, the pantie part insisted on riding diagonally up on my butt, creating four cheeks instead of two. And when I leaned over in my sultriest "Hey, Big Guy" pose, my boobs fell out, looking like sad sock puppets dangling over the top of my teddy. Gave that one to my DIL.

6. Power Mama. A big ol' spandex pantie with a maternity panel. No need to try this one, because… well, fifty-eight. But I gained sixty-five pounds when I was pregnant, and my only question is, *where the hell was this in 1989*?

I now have a drawer full of slimmers and shapers that, I admit, I rarely wear. But I did hear that Spanx is considering a long-sleeved, full-length, turtleneck version. I'm getting one in every color.

CHAPTER 31

And That's Why Parents Invented the Stork Story

"I want to have children, but my friends scare me. One of my friends told me she was in labor for 36 hours. I don't even want to do anything that feels good for 36 hours."
—Rita Rudner

"GRANDMA, ARE YOU DADDY'S MOM?"

I looked down at my six-year-old grandson's beautiful eyes staring up at me, his little brow slightly furrowed as he tried to get his family tree sorted out·in his mind. "Yes." I smiled, while silently praying, *Dear God, please, don't let this question go any further.*

But God was apparently taking another call, because the little guy thought for a moment and asked, "If Daddy was in your tummy, how did he get out?" *Oh, crap.*

Time stood still as my brain replayed my experience of bringing young grasshopper's daddy into the world, and the movie highlights included a few indelible moments:

—**I gained sixty-five pounds.** And I'm five-foot three inches tall. My baby hump was so big, I was ultrasound-scanned twice for twins. Doc said there simply *had* to be two babies in there. Nope. I was just fat. Of course, to be fair, I hoovered frosted brownies like they were life support, obviously thinking I was going to have a sixty-five-pound baby, so it was a nine-month eating free-for-all. (My size-two sister took one horrified look at my pre-birthing photo and asked, "Were you really that *hungry?* Or is this some kind of freaky hormonal thing?" My mother still blames me for Sissy opting not to have children.)

—**At my Lamaze class,** the instructor was speaking about birth control after the first few months post-birth. I raised my hand and asked, "What about the first three months?" which promptly sent seasoned birthers into peals of group laughter. "Oh, honey," one woman replied, wiping her eyes, "this must be your first. For the first three to four months, birth control is 'Get off me.'" Good to know.

—**At a New Year's Eve party**, when I was seven months into what felt like a two-year pregnancy (elephants give birth in less time... true story), we ran smack into Hubs's ex-girlfriend, a tiny, just-too-perky-for-words aerobics instructor with a killer body. She was wearing a skirt *almost* longer than her woo-hoo, with a midriff-baring top, and four-inch stilettos (seriously, girl: *put some clothes on*), while I was wearing a pup tent with matching flats. And since my hair wouldn't take a color from day one of my pregnancy, it had returned to its natural rodent-brown shade, so I was in a pup tent with matching flats *and* rodent-colored hair. We left early, with me bawling all the way home.

—**My due date came and went**, and I was getting so depressed, my mom suggested pedicures to help pass the time. Upon arrival, the nail tech announced, "Are you *sure*? You look like you're going to have that baby now." "I'm *never* going to have this baby," I replied. "I'm going to be pregnant until I die. Let's do this." We happily got soaked, scrubbed, and polished; then I stood up, and my water broke. Seriously? All instructions to my OB/GYN to "mind the wet toes" were blithely ignored.

—**Hubs finally showed up** with my overnight bag and a copy of my birthing plan. Since I was only going to do this once, I wanted it to be perfect. Part of "perfect" meant *no drugs*. This was going to be a serene, life-changing, mystical event that bonded mother and child like the biblical Madonna and her baby. Yeah, no. I was in labor forty-five hours. Again, not a typo. Forty. Five. Hours. The nurses had four shift changes while I was there, each time coming into the room with, "*What*, girl? You're *still here*?" Well, not by choice, lady. This kid keeps changing his mind and crawling back up the chute. The birthing plan got "accidentally" shredded while I demanded, and got, enough drugs to induce endless hours of enthusiastic, but widely off-key, renditions of "I met him on a Sunday and my heart stood still. Da doo run run run, da doo run run." Yep, I sucked at parenting, and the kid wasn't even born yet.

—**By the 45th hour,** Doc was prepping to do a cesarean section, when one of the nurses shouted, "I can see his head!!" You don't know humble until two doctors, eight nurses, your husband, your parents, and some guy I'm pretty sure was the night janitor, are all staring up your skirts, excitedly pointing to something trying to come out of your body, and *you don't care.* I was exhausted, I had no dignity left, my throat was hoarse from days of singing, and I was *done.*

Besides the "no drugs" instruction in my now-defunct three-page birthing plan, I'd also stipulated "no forceps." Women have been popping kids out for centuries without help. How hard could it be? But my tiny offspring had apparently set up camp in my uterus and was planning on staying right where he was. Finally, Doc took my face in his hands and said, "If you don't push, I'm going to have to use forceps." I looked at him and mumbled sleepily, "I don't care if you use a freakin' ice cream scooper. I'm done. Get him out yourself."

Two days later, we proudly took home a beautiful, perfect, bouncing baby boy, and I was besotted for life. But as I looked down at my grandson's trusting face, I smiled and said, "You know what? Let's go read a book. Grandma knows a great story called 'Hansel & Gretel.'" Yeah, it's about a witch in the forest that kidnaps children, bakes them in an oven, and then eats them. But I figure it'll require less childhood therapy than the story of how Daddy came to be.

CHAPTER 32

23 Things Anne Lander Could Have Learned From my Mother

"Sooner or later, we all quote our mothers."
—Bern Williams

I WAS ELEVEN WHEN my mom and stepdad got married. Both parents had three kids, so the marriage instantly turned us into a large, boisterous family trying to learn to live together and share *everything*, with each child constantly jockeying for position and attention from the clearly-exhausted and constantly-outflanked new stepparents from either side.

My stepdad was a doctor, so he sought refuge at his clinic and the local hospital, where he could be in charge with no questions asked (this was in the late sixties, where doctors told God what to do). Mom stayed home with the kids. Within the next couple of years, five out of the six were teenagers. *All at the same time.* There was a reason 5 p.m. was referred to as "Attitude Adjustment Hour" at our house.

My mother quickly developed a parenting style that was pithy, blunt, and on-the-fly. She had no time for silliness like drawn-out negotiating or soul-searching chats with her offspring, biological or otherwise. Mom would drop tidbits of wisdom like bread crumbs, and if we were smart, we'd listen. If we were *really* smart, we'd learn.

Like many women, after raising my own child and then handed darling, dimpled grandchildren to help guide along life's journey, I find myself repeating maternal admonitions recalled from my youth. The older I get, the smarter Mom was. So this chapter is dedicated to my mother and her Most Memorable Mom-isms.

1. If you're fighting with someone you care about, be the first to say "I'm sorry." You don't have to *mean* it. You just have to *say* it. (Well, *somebody* has to go first.)

2. It's time to diet when you're wider from the side view than from the front. Weirdly accurate. It's better than a scale. Go look. We'll wait.

3. The only way 2 people can keep a secret is if one of them is dead. We thought she invented "I'd tell you, but then I'd have to kill you." To this day, you can't coax, bribe, or threaten a secret out of any of us.

4. The best way to avoid falling in love with a poor man is not to date one. Mom was nothing if not practical.

5. If you kiss a boy, he'll want to "do it", and you'll get pregnant. Granted, we were very young, but for years my sisters and I thought kissing made you pregnant. Mom's work was done.

6. Absence makes the heart grow fonder. For someone else. By the time we were all in college, this became, "Absence makes the heart realize it doesn't miss your absent ass."

7. Don't confuse the wedding with the marriage. Mama Kardashian might have done better by her daughters if she'd have passed this one down.

8. A woman rarely regrets *not* sleeping with a man. The same can't be said of the opposite. In our younger days, it was a more direct: "Keep your knees together and your feet on the floor." That worked, too.

9. You can learn a lot about a man by how he treats his dog. Mom nailed this one. It's true. Every. Time.

10. Marriages are like pancakes. You usually screw the first one up. With six kids and fourteen marriages divided between us, we might have taken this one a bit too literally. Don't judge.)

11. Don't buy a car you haven't driven or marry a man you haven't slept with. They're both hard to return. I was in my twenties by this time. And it *was* the '80s.

12. Frankly, Scarlett, you're not that important. Instantly squashed all wails of "Everybody will be looking at me!" when we got a zit on prom night.

13. You can't be the bride at every wedding or the corpse at every funeral. We learned "It's not always about *you*" very early. Nice job, Mom.

14. If he says he's not good enough for you, he's right. "You're too good for me" became the relationship kiss of death with the girls in my family. See ya', buddy.

15. Fred was good, but Ginger did it all backwards. In stilettos. Be Ginger. Did I mention that Mom was a rebel?

16. Never be a mistress. You'll either get dumped or become his wife, in which case he'll get a new mistress. Usually emphasized with a finger shake and "You following me here?"

17. Promiscuous men are studs. Promiscuous women are tramps. Men don't marry tramps. They may sleep with them, but they don't marry them. Self-explanatory and undisputed.

18. Life is not fair. Deal with it. (See #17)

19. Don't smoke. But if you must, do so only when seated. Women who walk while smoking look trashy. Surprisingly true. Check it out next time you're in a mall.

20. Never do anything for a man when you're dating that you don't want to do for him when you're married. It sets a nasty precedent. So to all the boyfriends I never cooked for, blame Mom.

21. Assume every photo of you will be seen by me, your dad, your minister, your boss, and your future children. All aspirations of becoming Porn Star Patti in college instantly vaporized. Go, Mom.

22. Never bet on a horse with a bad track record. Usually accompanied by a stern look and an admonition, "If he lies and cheats on you, he's a jerk. But if you let him, you're an idiot. I didn't raise idiots."

23. When in doubt, be fabulous. And we were.

Thanks, Mom, for your wit and your wisdom. Despite what must have not-infrequently seemed insurmountable odds, you raised some pretty terrific (and occasionally fabulous) kids. And now I'm going to get my granddaughter. We're going to have a talk about kissing.

CHAPTER 33
17 Fashion Trends I'd Like to See Die

"If you have to ask if an item or clothing is a dress or a top, it's always a top."
—Tim Gunn

I LOVE FASHION. Clothes, shoes, boots, accessories, handbags... all shiny and new, promising if not actually a *better* life, certainly a better-dressed one.

One of the benefits of aging is the discovery of what works for you and what doesn't. We're less easily manipulated by the fashion industry into buying clothes that are unflattering, silly, or just plain stupid. We understand our bodies, what we want to show off, and what we would prefer to keep between ourselves and our bathroom mirrors.

But there are some fashion statements that don't work for *anybody* and that need to be taken out behind the barn and shot. How they originally came to be is simple. New trends are continuously streamed to the public, so stores can continue to sell clothes. After all, who needs a new black skirt if the one you bought last year is still in style?

But *why* they remain prevalent is often a mystery. Occasionally, even the designers are baffled. They know a trend is universally horrible, but they assume it'll sell out quickly and be replaced next season with another new must-have. Sometimes the designers are wrong.

Following is my list of Fashion Trends I'd Like to See Die:

1. Low-rise jeans on most women. Low-rise jeans introduced the concept of muffin top. When your waistband cuts straight across the middle of your belly (the trouble spot on millions of women worldwide), it's going to squish the excess fat up and over the top. There's simply nowhere else for it to go. *And* every time you lean over, we all get to see the Great Crevice, often highlighted by your hot pink thong that has crept up your butt crack and now lies snuggled in the roll above your jeans.

2. Low-rider gang banger jeans on men. This is the longest-running male trend *ever*, and it's hideous. This one continues to baffle me, since it was originally developed by convicted felons who used it as a prison mating call to show their availability to other inmates. Guys, you don't look tough. You look like an idiot who needs to pull up his damn britches (and this means you, Mr. Bieber).

3. Crocs. Yep, I'm still seeing these. I recently saw a bright orange pair on a fifty-something gentleman. With socks. Some things can't be unseen. If you're over the age of four (or a male at *any* age), for the love of God, toss these.

4. Nail art. It's just tacky. While it can be cute on little girls who want flowers on their tiny pink nails, if you're old enough to vote and you simply must have daisies painted on your nails to celebrate spring, put them on your toes.

5. French manicures. These are so *over*. They've been around for thirty years, and they're tired. Even Tim Gunn remarked that once you've seen a trend take over every trailer park in town, it's time to let it go.

6. Tights worn as pants. When leggings became hot, apparently people became confused about what actually constitutes pants. Leggings are heavier and more opaque, providing the same coverage as pants, just skinnier. Tights are much sheerer, clearly showing the rest of us your cellulite, your underwear, and your lady bush. Huge difference. *Huge.*

7. Camo print. Especially in pink. If you want to look like a soldier, join the military. Even if you're a shotgun-toting, mud-wrestling, female trucker with a gun rack, this is a tough look to pull off. And adding in a pink motif just makes you look confused.

8. High-low skirts and dresses. Above the knees in front, draping down to the floor in back. Fashionistas call this a "mullet skirt." 'Nuf said.

9. Any item sporting a logo from the Hello Kitty Collection on any woman old enough to be called "ma'am."

10. Printed tights. Looney Tunes, skulls, food products, black-and-white checks, stripes: all guaranteed to make the average woman's butt look the size of a freeway billboard. Unless you're an anorexic gazelle, pass on these.

11. Uggs boots with shorts. It's unclear who originally decided to pair sheepskin boots with shorts, but it looks stupid. Leave this one to the high schoolers. They're young enough to look silly and still be cute.

12. Harem pants. Looking for an extra ten pounds, stumpy legs, and a saggy ass? Look no further. The rest of you, *run*.

13. Cropped tops on women over thirty. I don't care how thin or fit you are. Too MILFY, and not enough class. And worn with low-rise jeans? I'm betting your T-shirt says *Honk if You Think I'm Hot*.

14. Cheap Faux leather. It looks like vinyl. And many women, inexplicably, like to wear this in one size smaller than they actually are, which, unfortunately makes you look like an overstuffed sausage, ready to explode at any minute and take out the room.

15. Peplums. Flares of gathered fabric on a jacket or dress that lie on your hips or butt. These make supermodels look hippy. The female version of the fanny pack.

16. Sweat pants as "real pants." Unless you're in college and your only concern is comfort, these are just *wrong*. Think Pajama Jeans, but baggier. With elastic waistbands. Bulky, shapeless, and unflattering. The trifecta of "What the hell was I *thinking*?"

17. Mini-skirts on women over forty. Even if you're thin enough to pull it off, it lacks class. And worn bare-legged or in denim, it'll rocket you from MILF to tramp before you can put on that third coat of mascara. Unless you're Tina Turner, at forty-plus your T-shirts should cover your navel and your skirts should cover your vagina.

Now, if you're wailing, "But I *love* my camo pants!" remember: this is just one woman's opinion. If you can rock the Hello Kitty faux leather jacket with matching nail decals, keep on going with your rebel self. I won't say a word.

•

•

CHAPTER 34
Goulash. It's What's For Dinner

"My second favorite household chore is ironing; my first being hitting my head on the top bunk bed until I faint."
—Erma Bombeck

I HAVE A THEORY about cooking. Despite what many people (particularly those who cook) claim, it's *not* simply a matter of "following the directions." Even the most rudimentary recipes love to toss around cooking terms that non-cooks struggle with. What *exactly* is a "pinch" of something? Would that be like a tiny, baby-cheek pinch? Or a big 'ol butt-grabbing pinch? And how much of something is a "smidgen"? Or a "skosh"? And every recipe includes at least one instruction to "sprinkle to taste." How the hell would I know, unless I lick the bowl as I go? Of course, if you *do* get actual measurements, they're often flexible. This doesn't work for us. "One-half to one tablespoon" just makes non-cooks crazy. *Which is it, dammit?* One half tablespoon or one tablespoon? It's *your* recipe. You tell *me*.

One year, Hubs made the unfortunate decision to get me an intimidating binder called *The Joy of Cooking*. (Yeah, like he got lucky *that* night.) *Every* recipe called for more ingredients than I have in my house in an entire year. After the third try of a ridiculously complicated side dish (got all the way to the bottom, where it read, "Pour sauce over top before serving. For sauce recipe, see page 322." *Seriously?*), I frisbee'd the stupid book out my back patio door and onto the soccer field next door. Poor thing got run over by a large rider mower and has now gone to confetti heaven, *where it belongs*.

My sister, however, is an award-winning chef and valedictorian of her culinary school. Magazines take photos of her food, and her menus are chosen for edibility and something called "presentation." Given the fact that the only pictures of anything I cook are on the front of the microwavable box it comes in, she is, to this day, convinced there was a hospital mix-up and her "real sister" is still out there. (I just keep telling her that some of us were born for other things, and I was born simply to be fabulous. She's not buying it and repeatedly asks my mother, "Are you *sure* she's ours?")

Finally taking pity on me (or Hubs, who lost fourteen pounds in our first year of marriage before he realized I *truly* couldn't cook), Sissy sent me her "EZ Lasagna" recipe. (Note to Sissy: "EZ" to Julia Child and "EZ" to "When in Doubt, Pop Tarts are Always an Option" are *not* the same thing).

First step, chop the onion. Halfway through it, I was crying so hard, I couldn't see my knife, and I sliced my hand open. Wrapped that up (hopefully before I bled into the sauce, but it was tomato, so I'm admitting nothing), and moved on to "simmering" (What number on the dial is "simmer?" Again, *specifics*, people!), which, no matter how low I went, spit and splat tomato sauce *everywhere*, including down the front of my favorite white shirt. Well, crap.

Then there's those damn noodles that need to be stirred while boiling. Without thinking it through, I reached in to stir them with a short fork, plunging my hand into the boiling water. Yeah, that hurt. Tried pulling the cooked noodles apart to layer them in the lasagna pan, burning my two remaining undamaged fingers and shredding the noodles. Oh, screw it. Promptly dumped the entire mess into one pan, baked it for forty-five minutes, and told Hubs it was Hungarian Goulash.

Delighted with the fact that I'd cooked anything at all, he happily scarfed it down, while I was downing three ibuprofens and an entire bottle of wine. Dinner is served.

CHAPTER 35

You Called? 14 Reasons I Didn't Pick Up

*"Utility is when you have one telephone. Luxury is when you have two.
Opulence is when you have three, and paradise is when you have none."*
—Doug Larson

A FRIEND RECENTLY CALLED ME, upset because she got a $350 ticket for talking on her cell phone while driving. "It was *important*," she wailed. But it seemed no amount of explaining would convince Officer Do-Right that the need to move her massage appointment from 2:00 to 4:00 constituted an emergency.

Cell phones have changed the way we communicate with family, friends, co-workers, and even spouses. Twenty-something newlyweds text each other *while in the same room*. Couples have proposed or divorced via text messages.

But of all the changes we see cell phones making in our culture (including the apocalyptic demise of grammar and spelling), one of the most significant is that we've somehow come to expect twenty-four-hour availability from anyone on our speed dial list.

In the old days (yeah, anything before 2005), people would leave messages on answering machines and wait patiently for a return call that evening or even the next day. We understood that people had lives and were not attached to their phones like portable oxygen tanks. But we've gradually come to expect that, if you have a cell phone, you're expected to answer every call and return every text message *right freaking now*.

So today, I'm offering up my list of 14 Reasons (no matter how crazy I am about you or that we've been friends since 1963) I Might Not Pick Up When You Call.

1. I'm in the shower. It's hard to hear under a waterfall, and my phone insurance doesn't cover water damage (or stupidity, like, say, taking your cell phone into the shower).

2. I'm in a restaurant. People who have normal-volume conversations with someone across the table will pick up their cell phone and start shouting loudly enough to be heard in Botswana. Yes, the caller can hear you, but so can everyone else for six blocks in any direction.

3. I'm at work, and my crazy boss assumes my phone conversations will be about, well… work. (But, if those fabulous boots we saw last weekend are now on sale, text me.)

4. I'm driving. If you don't have $350 worth of news, leave a message, and I'll call you at the next truck stop.

5. I'm having a massage. Yep, as in naked, lying on a warm table, incense burning and a CD of crashing waves, all working together with a massage designed to bring the Feng back to my Shui, totally obliterated by your multiple redials simply to remind me to pick up some creamer for your coffee.

6. I'm having sex. In the movies, they always stop and pick up. *Seriously?* My phone has sailed out the window, been tossed down the hall, and, one time, thrown under my car. (Don't ask.) Even during bad sex (Bahahahaha! I crack myself up), in which case we're going back into the bedroom until we get it right. I'll get back to you tomorrow.

7. I'm on the potty. I've never been one to pee and chat simultaneously. And if it's a long conversation, does one flush while talking (which can be heard by the person on the other end, forever outing you as a toilet talker)? Or do you come back and flush after you both hang up? Social etiquette sites don't address this one, so I'll call you back when I'm done, okay?

8. I'm going through airport security. These people are cranky monkeys (particularly after being yelled at by pissed-off travelers all day long), and when they say "Ma'am, put that phone down *now*," unless you have an unfulfilled fantasy about being strip-searched while the contents of your luggage get tossed around like a fruit salad, you should just Put. The. Phone. Down.

9. I'm writing. Even Hubs knows to stay clear unless the house is on fire *and* it's reached the hallway. Otherwise, wait until I come out, all bleary-eyed and brain dead from four hours of editing my latest draft post. Too often, a great thought is working its way into a post but irretrievably vaporizes after a ten-minute phone chat about where to meet for lunch.

10. I'm getting a tattoo. No, I've never had one, but I can see the unfortunate result of leaning over to grab your phone while Mr. Nasty Needle is filling in the exotic bloom on your left breast, which now looks less like a bird of paradise and more like a really long party favor.

11. I'm at the gym. It's obvious that the guy on the treadmill next to mine, who has been arguing with his wife (apparently named "You Bitch," because he's been calling her that for the last forty-five minutes), seems to believe that we're all either deaf and can't hear them as they loudly resolve which one of them had an affair first, or that we *can* hear and are fascinated by their dramatic, reality-TV life.

12. I'm getting a Pap smear or a mammogram. In the first, all I can do is peer over the sheet to see a couple of people seriously focused on my lady parts; and in the second, I'm pretty much out of the game, because my breast is firmly sandwiched between two metal plates. Both positions effectively prevent any movement on my part, up to and including reaching for my phone.

13. I'm watching a movie. I prefer movies to TV shows because I don't like interruptions (after the seventh senior-incontinence commercial, I lose the plot and the mood). I tend to turn my phone off for movies, even if it *is* the seventeenth viewing of *The Notebook*.

14. I'm at a wedding (or any other significant event). Looking coy and slightly embarrassed when your phone goes off during someone's wedding vows is only slightly less rude than actually answering it and getting up to leave the service, with an audible whisper, "I'm sorry, but I've got to take this." If you're that busy and important, skip the service and send a card.

So, excluding family members with unresolved anger issues who feel the need to vent (*again*), my stalker ex-boyfriend who still believes we're destined to be together, or the persistent English-as-a-ninth-language sales guy with the condo in Rio you'll sell me for half price because, dammit, I *deserve* it (in which case, I'll get back to you, yeah, never), I promise to return your call as soon as I'm not doing any of the above activities.

In the meantime, as they say, "Your call is very important to me. Please leave a message, and I'll get back to you as quickly as I can."

CHAPTER 36

"Not Tonight, Dear, I Have a Headache."
What is She Really Saying?

"A woman's rule of thumb: If it has tires or testicles, you're going to have trouble with it."
—Unknown

IN ANY LONG-TERM RELATIONSHIP, regardless of the love and commitment of the two people involved, sexual desire is going to ebb and flow. Experts assure us it's normal•and natural. Desire can be impacted by stress, hormones, illness or medications, foods we're eating, alcohol intake, and a host of other human conditions or behaviors, and doesn't automatically indicate trouble in the relationship.

If a man is not in the mood, it becomes quickly apparent to both parties. It's just not happening, and so we return to our previous activities, tacitly agreeing never to speak of it again.

Women, however, have a few options if the mood strikes our partner but we're not feeling it at that moment. We can either confess our temporary loss of interest (often igniting a twenty-minute debate about how we'll undoubtedly change our minds "once we get into it"), be accommodating and fake it, or claim the proverbial "headache."

"Not tonight, dear, I have a headache" is the time-honored, classic get-out-of-sex card for women around the globe, primarily because it can't be argued. Simply put, you can't prove that she doesn't.

But what's really behind "the headache"? If she never gets headaches at any other time and doesn't have a brain tumor, it's not unreasonable to conclude that there's another explanation to her lack of enthusiasm for a quickie on the kitchen table.

•

Assuming you're not a complete douche who thinks that midnight groping while she's asleep or grabbing her boobs whenever she walks past you on her way to the laundry room constitutes foreplay, and that she didn't have sex earlier in the day with someone else, doesn't have any health issues and all is well in hoo-hoo world, and that if she *did* want sex, you'd be the default partner of choice, there are myriad reasons why she'd play the headache card that don't automatically indicate the permanent evaporation of her desire for your awesomeness.

1. She's having a self-esteem meltdown, brought on by a day of swimsuit shopping and fluorescent lighting on her back fat and sudden-onset thigh cellulite; even if you could talk her out of her clothes, she'll come to bed wearing a burka.

2. It's only been three minutes since you started the massage you've been promising to give her for a week, and now you're stripping your clothes off like a drunk sailor on shore leave, eager to "get this party started." Sometimes a massage just needs to be a massage.

3. The fight you had last night isn't over and she's still pissed. Those stupid, quasi-rape scenes on TV where the couple is screaming at each other until he slams her up against the wall and goes all caveman until she finally submits with a sigh are *fiction*. If her comments to you indicate remaining hostility ("Dinner's ready, Jackass"), back up and get your hands off of her lady parts.

4. Last night, you went out together and you paid attention to everybody but her. "But we see each other all the time" may be true, but ditching her at the door then spending the entire evening yucking it up with two old football buddies and the big-breasted cocktail waitress with the cropped *With Love From Hooters* T-shirt is guaranteed to get your inconsiderate butt shoved to the opposite side of the bed for the rest of the night.

5. You've been in a crappy mood all day long and have been taking it out on her, even though you told her it "has nothing to do with her." That's swell, but at the end of the day, she'll want nothing to do with *you*.

6. You've been watching football all day in your baggy sweats, drinking beer and eating chips, belching out the national anthem before every game, and surprisingly, she's just not turned on.

7. **Everybody and their family goat has been wanting something from her all day long.** Her boss needs her to work on Saturday, the kids need to get to piano and soccer (at opposite ends of town), the house looks like a war zone and your mother is coming for the weekend, laundry is piled up, the washing machine has inexplicably died, and the dog just puked on the couch. She just wants to be left *alone*. The best thing you could do is bring her a bottle of wine and some chocolate. Then go away.

8. **You waited until she was showered, dressed, made-up, and on her way out the door to give her "the wink."** Seriously, dude? You couldn't have thought of this an hour ago?

9. **You're sweaty and dirty, and you smell bad.** We're thrilled that you're feeling all pumped up from your great racquet ball game or installing the back deck, but take a shower first, m'kay?

10. **She just walked in the door,** everyone is hungry, her mother has called three times with instructions to call her back ASAP, her feet are throbbing from the heels she's been wearing for nine hours, she's exhausted and just needs a moment to relax and *breathe*. "You can do all that later" isn't helpful and will most likely result in her thinking about her To-Do list the entire time you're busting your best bedroom moves.

11. **You're drunk and she's not.** While we love that you have a posse to go out with and watch endless months of sports bowls and playoffs over bottomless pitchers of beer, coming home gassed at midnight with your drunk frisky on is just not foreplay.

12. **You only touch her when you're horny.** And you assume that any and all touching from *her* automatically indicates a spontaneous desire get naked and jump your bones. We like to feel attractive and desirable even with our clothes *on*. We're funny like that.

13. **She's just not feeling it** and doesn't want to have to fake it.

14. **You're doing it wrong, and she's afraid to tell you.** And you haven't asked.

So next time she claims a headache, ask if that's *truly* the reason. Or better yet, go unload the dishwasher. You'd be surprised what turns us on.

CHAPTER 37

Today I Fired My BFF

"A positive attitude may not solve all your problems, but it will annoy enough people to make it all worth the effort."
—Herm Albright

I RECENTLY READ AN INTERESTING article about self-talk and the things we say to ourselves every day. Apparently, therapists generally agree that if Hubs or a friend spoke to us the way we speak to *ourselves*, we'd kick them to the curb right freaking now. (Okay, I paraphrased.)

The writer pointed out that, since the person we spend the most time with every day is, well, *us*, that's where most of our personal feedback comes from. A co-worker who remarks, "Gee, that skirt is a little tight, don't you think?" doesn't do near as much damage to our self-esteem as a daily inner mantra, repeatedly chanting to ourselves, *Yep, you're still fat.*

The brain believes what it's told, so it's critical that we become aware of the constant barrage of judgmental, belittling "truths" that we unconsciously tell ourselves all day long. In short, we need to be our own biggest cheerleaders. Our own best friends.

She suggested an experiment where you journal your conversations with yourself over the course of a day, to see what kind of a friend you are to *you*. Here's what I found. (Meet my inner voice, "BBF," or Bad Best Friend):

1. The morning weigh-in:

Me: "Staying down where it should. This isn't so hard."

BBF: "Yeah, since you haven't eaten dinner in *a week*. You won't last. If you had that kind of control, you wouldn't have been a Teletubby in the first place. Same time tomorrow, Porkchop."

2. Out of the shower, naked inspection:

Me: "Not bad for fifty-eight. With a push-em-up bra and Spanx, I could still work it."

BBF: "You're kidding, right? Then what's that on the back of your thighs? That's it, bend over, look between your thighs, and tell me what you see. Yep, it's your *sagging butt cheeks*. They evidently thought your boobs looked lonely, so they joined them on the Gravity Express. Still feel like 'working it'?"

3. Blow-drying my hair:

Me (holding up blow-dryer): "My triceps need a little toning. Maybe I'll get one of those Shake Weights."

BF: "Yeah, that'll work. If you're *twelve*. That wobbling skin under your arms is called 'turkey waddle,' and it's only sexy on poultry. Now you'll be wearing long sleeves in July, just like all the other middle-aged grandmothers in the park."

4. Makeup:

Me: "My skin looks pretty good. Must be good genes. A little tinted moisturizer to smooth it out, and I'm ready to go."

BBF: "Who are you kidding? You've had an eye job *and* Botox, and you still have a L.A. road map around your eyes. And is that a *chin hair* I see??"

5. Getting dressed:

Me: "This dress would look better over Spanx, but it's too hot, so not today. I look fine."

BBF: "Yeah, if your definition of 'fine' is a fifty-eight-year old woman with ass-jiggle when *she's standing still*. No Spanx, no dress, lady."

6. Career:

Me: "Got to get to work. But someday I'm going to make a living by writing."

BBF: "Dream on, baby. So far, you've only impressed your mother and an ex-boyfriend from high school, class of 1974. And if you ever *do* actually write a book, your mother is going to expect a free copy. Don't quit your day job, you hack."

7. Dieting:

Me: "I'm going to lose two pounds this week. I'm committed. Where's the produce department?"

BBF: "Yeah, how would you know? You haven't eaten a vegetable in, like, fifty-eight years. And you might want to take the giant box of Milk Duds, three frozen pizzas, Brown Cow Diet (*seriously*?) ice cream sandwiches, Doritos Fire Chips, and the six bottles of wine out of your cart. *You* on a diet? Bahahahaha!"

8. Shopping:

Me: "That bikini in the boutique window is so cute. I remember those days."

BBF: "Oh, please. You couldn't wear that in high school. Why do you think your parents always called you the 'wholesome one'? Get a clue, Blondie. That wasn't a compliment."

Me: "Fine, but look at that rockin' black leather jacket. Ooh, I could definitely do *that*."

BBF: "Absolutely, if you're going for aging, rock-band groupie. Why don't you just buy a leopard print miniskirt and a T-shirt that says *I Used to be Hot*?"

9. Grandkids:

Me: "I wish we lived closer to the kids so I could see them more often."

BBF: "Yeah, I'll bet that's what they're thinking, too. 'Gee, we wish Mom was here every day, so she could be all up in our business and give us lots of advice on how we spend our money and how to raise our kids. That would be way cool.'"

10. Out and About:

Me: "That delightful young man behind the counter is smiling at me."

BBF: (*Snort*) "Uh, look behind you. See that hot twenty-something blonde gazelle in the cropped top? I'm betting it was *her*, not you. Besides, you could be that boy's mother and not have been a child bride, if you get my drift. Guys who flirt with you aren't called 'guys.' They're called 'seniors,' and they carry AARP cards, not backpacks."

11. Dinner:

Me: "No, I'm not going to eat dinner tonight. If I have more than a Fruit Loop and a Diet Coke after 5:00, my weight goes up. But I'm disciplined. I'll pass tonight."

BBF: "Ha! By the second glass of wine, you'll be hitting the Pringles *hard*. Admit defeat now, snarf down that pizza, and kick yourself in the morning, like every morning, Chubs."

It seems that my inner best friend is kind of a bitch.

That night, I sent her a text.

Dear Bad Best Friend,

You know this friendship thing? You suck at it. So get on down the road with your judgmental, mean-girl self, because I'm dumping your ass. When you can say "Good morning, Gorgeous" without rolling your eyes and snorting, we'll discuss reconciliation possibilities. Until then, I will no longer consult you on any matters pertaining to my worth.

I feel more confident already. And now, if you'll excuse me, there's a fabulous black leather jacket that's calling my name.

•

CHAPTER 38

It Could've Been Worse.
I Could've Been Wearing a Thong.

"Midlife has hit you when you stand naked in front of a mirror and you can see your rear end without turning around."
—Unknown

HOOD RIVER, OREGON is a beautiful, resorty-type destination town, nestled between the base of Mt. Hood and the Columbia River. In the spring and summer, tourist season quadruples our population, as hordes of visitors descend on our small community to part with piles of cash as they stroll the waterfront and check out the outdoor cafés, homemade ice cream shops, multiple wine-tasting rooms, expensive boutiques, and local art galleries.

I worked for several years in an upscale women's clothing and beauty boutique, smack in the middle of the downtown core. As the Beauty Director, it was my job to convince the throngs of female shoppers who packed our little store all summer long that they truly couldn't *live* another day without that wildly expensive moisturizer ($171 *per jar*, and I couldn't stock it fast enough), while my sales partner was happily wrapping up the $700 python boots that Chelsea from Montana just *had* to have. By the end of each day, we were both "peopled out" and ready to go home for a non-tourist-priced glass (okay, three) of wine.

Before we left each night, we'd spend twenty to thirty minutes getting everything cleaned up and properly displayed for the next morning. This included dusting, wiping, steaming and re-hanging, plus finally vacuuming the hardwood. We'd lock up, turn the stereo up *LOUD* to something fun ("All the Single Ladies" got a *lot* of air time one particular year), and shake off the day by singing and dancing our way around the store, busting our goofiest moves while performing quite possibly the world's worst karaoke. We were God-awful, but we were enthusiastic.

One evening, as I was running the vacuum cleaner hose along the front of the store, belting out something about "puttin' a ring on it" while waving my arms to the beat, the hose suddenly caught the edge of my dress and, despite my frantic attempts to pull it out, instantly sucked up my dress clear up to my waist. By the time I reached the *Off* switch, I was standing in the window on the busiest street in town, at the peak of tourist season, between two mannequins, wearing what now appeared to be only a T-shirt, a pair of Spanx, and a mortified expression.

To the three drivers who rear-ended each other while watching the whole thing play out (whose expressions were decidedly more "Oh. Dear. God." than "Yeah, baby!") and to the latte-sipping guys on the sidewalk doubled over in apparently uncontrollable hilarity, yes, I realize I'm a few decades past my best mooning days. And to the horrified mother with the two wide-eyed toddlers, send me a bill for their therapy. The check is in the mail.

CHAPTER 39
24 Things Women Want in the Pre-Nup
(No, They're Not About Money.)

"Can you imagine a world without men? No crime and lots of fat, happy women."
—Marion Smith

HUBS AND I RECENTLY SPENT a delightful evening having dinner out with friends, and someone commented on yet another ninety-minute Hollywood marriage that was on the rocks; both parties were currently in court in a headline-making battle over the validity of the pre-nup. Apparently it takes eight lawyers and a judge to determine the actual legal definition of "cheating."

Amidst much wine-induced hilarity over the fact that our four incomes combined wouldn't get any of us within 100 miles of a pre-nup zip code, the women began to formulate a list of what *we* would have included, if we'd presented a pre-nup to our current spouses before we were married oh-so-many years ago.

Most couples talk freely and endlessly about the big issues, like whether or not to have children and, if so, how many; religious beliefs; city vs. country living; merging finances; how to handle crazy in-laws, ex-spouses and stepchildren; divergent career paths and whose comes first. But these are rarely the things that topple a relationship.

It's the *little things* that really matter. The day-to-day annoyances that build up over time until someone comes home to find their entire vintage CD collection out in the front yard and the locks changed on the master bedroom door. Experts say that finances and sex problems are the two greatest causes of divorce. I say it's continuing to leave your dirty laundry on the bathroom floor and drinking the last of the coffee before she's even out of the shower—

after she's complained about both for *years* — that ultimately start to piss her off until she threatens to leave your uncooperative and oblivious ass for the UPS guy.

So, in the interest of promoting marital harmony, I've compiled a list of *25 Things Women Want in the Pre-Nup* that will help keep the waters of marital bliss smooth and untroubled for years to come.

1. Repeatedly leaving the toilet seat up is the male equivalent of the female "Not tonight, dear. I have a headache." It means nobody's getting any tonight.

2. Borrowing my car and returning it with the gas gauge on "E" tells me it's been too long since we've had a good fight.

3. Drinking the last Diet Coke without replacing my stash is exactly the same as me letting your beer fridge run dry.

4. Three hours of trying to get your attention and actually talk to you, while you scream and yell at the TV during the entire course of the Big Game, is not "spending time together."

5. No, I cannot stay at my hot pre-wedding weight and eat a big dinner with you every night. You're going to have to choose.

6. Yes, I know you hate the songs on my iPod. That's why they call it an "I" Pod. Get your own.

7. Beer is not the only liquid that will quench your thirst.

8. Just because you were born with a penis doesn't mean you automatically know how to fix my car. We're hiring a mechanic.

9. Throwing all my delicates into the dryer on *High* isn't "helping with the laundry."

10. There is no official religious sanction in any recognized church that prohibits putting the new toilet paper roll *on the dispenser* rather than on the bathroom counter. I checked.

11. Blaring surround-sound in a tiny living room is not "way cool." It's just loud. I don't need to hear helicopters behind my head.

12. There isn't a woman alive, in any country on the planet, who thinks "fine" is a synonym for "beautiful." When you say "You look fine" or "That dress is fine," I guarantee you that we just heard, "You look boring and plain, but I'm getting impatient, so let's go." And the next time you ask "Was it good for you?" we'll respond, "It was fine."

13. After two arm whacks and a swift kick in the shins, if you're still snoring, I'm sleeping in the guest bedroom. Yes, I still love you.

14. **No, you cannot wear your neon, tie-dyed T-shirt from college to dinner with my parents.** Or at any event we attend together. Ever.

15. **I don't care if we've shared a toothbrush from time to time, when you drink milk directly out of the container, it has backwash in it, and I can't drink it.** Same for my Diet Cokes. The glasses are in the cabinet on the left side of the fridge.

16. **Thong underwear feels like dental floss in your butt crack, and four-inch stilettos are as comfy as ballet toe shoes.** These were invented by men. You wear 'em.

17. **Yanking the duvet up over the still-wadded sheets and blankets is not "making the bed."**

18. The distance between your hand and the sink is roughly the same as that between your hand and the dishwasher, so all things being equal, **please put your dirty dishes in the dishwasher, not the sink.**

19. **We will never be married long enough for me to find ball-and-chain jokes funny.**

20. **If I'm wearing it, it's because I like it.** And if I like it, you like it. Yes, even the boyfriend jeans.

21. **If I ever ask, "You look fabulous" is the only correct response.** And why did I have to ask?

22. **Just because I do all the shopping doesn't mean I do all the spending.** The dry-cleaning I picked up was yours. The $40 moisturizer I bought at Nordstrom was yours. The dozen T-shirts from Target? Yours. You say "we" need to stop spending? You first.

23. **There are many great movies with no screaming car chase scenes, automatic weapons on constant firing, alien invasions, or apocalyptic backdrops.** We also like comedies, musicals, or even *love stories*. And spending the entire movie repeatedly asking, "When does anything *happen*?" or "Do they have to *sing* everything?" is virtually guaranteed to have us watching movies in different rooms of the house.

24. **A sports bar with unlimited "Buckets-O-Wings" and twenty-seven TVs will never be my choice for date night.** Or, actually, any night. Go. Have fun. I'll pick the next one. No TVs, but you'll love the wine list.

You're welcome.

CHAPTER 40

How to Make a Halloween Costume Without Spending a Dime

"For Halloween this year, I'm going as Karma. Some of you should be worried."
—Unknown

OKAY, I ADMIT IT. I'm a Halloween curmudgeon. I just don't get this day. It's an outdoor event, in late October, when it's invariably rainy, dark, and cold, primarily revolving around scaring the crap out of sugar-crazed herds of costumed tater tots, while simultaneously encouraging them to approach total strangers for candy (subsequently undoing years of stern lessons about "stranger danger").

Fifteen minutes into the relentless ringing of our doorbell, accompanied by shouts of *"TRICK OR TREAT!"* from shivering, masked children holding up pillowcases, demanding copious amounts of candy in exchange for not throwing food products at your house, our two Chihuahuas are set off into full-frenzy bark mode for the entire evening, ultimately necessitating doggy downers for either them or us. God help you if you run out of candy. Those sweet-faced little ladybugs get *pissed*. (And what's up with the teenagers? Drive up to your house, dressed like killer zombies in low-rider, oversized jeans and black hoodies, *trick-or-treating*? Screw that. They're casing the place.)

My greatest Halloween phobia is The Costume Party. The mere invitation sends my ADHD/OCD, Virgo Perfectionist, Overachieving Middle-Child Syndrome neuroses colliding at warp speed over *what to be*, until they eventually explode into a wine-chugging night of "For God's sake, woman, it's a *costume*. Just *PICK ONE*."

This year, I decided to get over my anxieties and try to make it fun. I poured a glass of wine and headed to down the hall to Google

"Most Popular Halloween Costumes" for ideas. Welcome to Hell. One look and I headed back to the kitchen for the rest of the bottle, returning to my office and settling in, determined to find something... *anything* I'd risk wearing in public if there was even the slightest possibility of running into an old boyfriend or my boss.

List of Top Choices from Google:

1. Sexy Witch. Who am I kidding? I'm a decade (*fine...* three decades) past black fishnets, stilettos, and pointy hats. There's a name for fifty-eight-year-olds who dress like that outside the bedroom, and it's not "hot."

2. Porky Pig. Essentially, a pink fleece adult onesie with a snout and eight plastic "teets." Yeah, no. After years of struggling with literally being the "bigger sister," I'll be damned if I'm going to wear anything resembling a pink sleeping bag or that includes the word "porky" in the description. *Ever.*

3. Toga. Not since the great Tri-Delt toga party debacle during my sorority years in 1978. Don't ask.

4. Naughty Nurse. By fifty-plus, this can be a little creepy and too suggestive of "Just happened to have this in my closet, right sweetie? (wink, wink)." Great idea until you run into your parents, your children (of any age), or your minister.

5. Catholic School Girl. See #4. Then imagine a short, plaid skirt and white knee-highs on a fifty-eight-year-old woman. Or don't. And does this mean Hubs dresses up as a pedophile on parole?

6. Fairy Princess. What am I? Like, nine? Besides, glitter on a middle-aged face settles into the lines, and sparkling, sagging cleavage is just *sad*.

7. Wonder Woman. Oh *hell*, no. If I won't wear a belted, sequined bustier with black panty-shorts and knee-high boots for Hubs (who's asked repeatedly), I'm certainly not going to wear them for the neighbors (who have, not surprisingly, never asked. Not once).

8. Miley Cyrus. Yeah, *there's* an idea. Dress up like a coked-out, wannabe rock star, with too much makeup, too little clothing, and zero sexual boundaries, whose primary claim to recent fame is the development of a new household word. And if you have to ask your children what "twerking" means, you're too old for this outfit, period.

9. Gogo Girl. This worked for Twiggy and Goldie Hawn in the early '70s. They were tall, anorexic, and twelve. I'm 5'3", curvy, and well, you get the idea. Besides, I grew up with "No white after Labor Day." Old habits are hard to break.

10. Mad Men Retro. This one requires all-night chain smoking, five-inch heels, and skirts you can't sit down in. I don't smoke, I have Parkinson's-induced balance issues, and wearing Spanx while snarfing down bowlfuls of candy is just stupid.

11. Jeannie (as in, "I Dream Of"). Oh, swell. Sheer, low-rise harem pants, with a sleeveless, see-through cropped top. This ensemble hides *nothing*. Boobs resemble wet sock puppets? Post-childbearing belly? A little chubbier than you were in, say, preschool? Put this outfit down and run, don't walk, to the nearest exit.

This was going to be tougher than I thought.

I finished my wine (yes, *all of it*), and decided to go as a fifty-eight-year-old writer, in bunny slippers, an oversized T-shirt, and faded yoga pants, who desperately needs to get off her computer and get to a gym, if for no other reason than to see daylight and real, live people, before friends and family succumb to rumors of her untimely demise and begin to send condolence cards.

No need to buy anything new. And I can take my laptop with me.

I could learn to like this holiday.

CHAPTER 41

How to Apologize to Your Wife

"An apology is the superglue of life. It can repair just about anything."
—Lynn Johnston

RECENTLY, OVER HOT TACOS and icy margaritas at our favorite local taco wagon, Hubs and I (and everyone else on the patio) overheard an argument between a young man and his wife that went from zero to sixty the instant he blurted out, "God, you sound just like your mother when you say that." She looked horrified and burst into tears. As she got up to leave, he smithereened any hope of working it out in the immediate future by calling out, "Sorry, I was *kidding*. I keep forgetting how sensitive you are."

Hubs grinned and winced, "Ouch. That poor idiot." The rest of us were thinking the same thing. Idiot guy better hope *his* mother hadn't yet turned his old bedroom into a home office, because he was going to be sleeping at Mom and Dad's for the next few nights.

All couples fight. You simply can't put two people in the same house for years on end and expect them to agree on every little thing, with neither of them ever, even inadvertently, saying or doing something stupid. One of the most important components in any relationship is the ability to suck it up and apologize when necessary. Apologizing is rarely comfortable or easy, but like most social graces, it can be learned.

Sometimes the best way to understand what works is to start with what *doesn't*.

1. Don't shift the blame. "I'm sorry you're so sensitive about your weight." Or, "I'm sorry you don't understand that men aren't programmed to remain faithful." This is the worst way to apologize since the dawn of mankind. You're telling her that *she's* the problem for getting pissed because *you* screwed up. Now you're fighting about two things instead of one. Good strategy.

2. Don't use the word "but." Ever. "I'm sorry I kissed your best friend, but *she* came onto *me*" is whiny and weak, suggesting that your only offense is the inability to resist temptation. So what you're saying is that you're a cheater with no balls.

3. Don't overcompensate. "I'm sorry. I'll never speak to that woman again" is stupid if "that woman" is her sister or works in your office. This isn't a solution. She knows you're just blowing her off and are done talking about it. Think of this one as the "white elephant" of apologies. Until you address it, it will always be in the room. And in the bed.

4. Don't dismiss it. "Sorry." Or worse, "My bad." Monosyllabic, non-explanatory apologies are thinly veiled attempts to get her to shut up and get over it already, and *she knows this*. Trust me, it *will* come up again, and your next fight is going to be a doozy.

5. Don't deflect. This is usually done with sarcasm. "Gee, I'm sorry. I'll be sure to *ask* next time before I go out drinking with the guys until midnight, just in case you had other plans for me," often accompanied by an eye roll. You're saying it's *her* fault for being so demanding and asking that you let her know if you're not coming home at the expected time. Fine. But the next time you stagger home drunk and seven hours late, be prepared for her to be out. And don't bother looking for a note.

6. Don't blame the alcohol. After age twenty, "I was drunk" excuses nothing. Alcohol releases inhibitions. It doesn't change who you are. If you're a douche when you're drunk, you're probably just basically a douche, period. Now she has two reasons to drop-kick your loser ass out the door.

7. Don't play dumb. "I don't know what I did wrong, but whatever it was, I'm sorry." By the time two people have been married for several years, each one knows *exactly* what sets the other one off. Looking confused but apologizing to pacify her makes you look like a child who denies eating all the cookies while his face is covered with chocolate. Man up, buddy.

8. Don't use the word "if." As in "I'm sorry if I hurt your feelings when I laughed at your cellulite." Or, "I'm sorry if I insulted your dog." *If?* We've spent the last hour dissecting what you did, and now we're back to *if* you actually did it? Bite me, jackass.

9. Don't apologize via cutesy email or, God forbid, a text. Because nothing says "I'm really, truly sorry I was a total tool and did something stupid that hurt you" than a free e-card with animated puppies or a shorthand phone text that says "Sry babe. Dnr out 2nite?" Leave these methods to the twenty-somethings. If you screwed up like an adult, apologize like one.

So what do you do when you've done what you did?

1. Acknowledge the offense and accept responsibility. "I'm sorry I didn't tell that waitress I was married and not interested."

2. Provide an explanation, not an excuse. Explanations provide a rationale for what you did. Excuses are juvenile reasons why it wasn't your fault. "I went to the strip club with my buddies because we were all drunk and it sounded good at the time" is better than, "I wasn't the driver, and that's where everybody else wanted to go, so what could I do?"

3. Express genuine remorse. Anyone who has ever been on the receiving end of a faux apology knows it when they hear one. A simple, but *sincere,* "I'm sorry" can melt the most unforgiving heart.

4. Offer a solution that prevents it from happening again. This one is a biggie. We need some reassurance that the offense won't become repetitive. "From now on, I will filter my comments at all events with your family, and I'll avoid any mention of your Aunt Bitsy's uncanny resemblance to her pot-bellied pig."

One of the best apology notes I've ever read summed it all up:

> *I apologize for decking your ex at your office Christmas party. He was hitting on you and I overreacted, embarrassing you in front of your boss and your co-workers. I apologize and promise it won't happen again. Next time, I'll go over to his house.*
>
> *Love,*
>
> *Hubs*

CHAPTER 42

Nice to Meet You. Who Does Your Botox?

"There are three periods in life: youth, middle age, and 'how well you look.'"
—Nelson Rockefeller

•

I WAS SITTING WITH A GROUP of girlfriends at our favorite local wine tasting room recently, getting caught up on our lives over lots of laughter, swapping gossip and sharing tips on families, work, shopping, and husbands, when the subject inevitably turned to *aging*...what we love (grandkids!) and what we hate (gravity).

Naturally, we immediately began collectively congratulating each other on how young we all look and how "fifty is the new forty." (How do you think we all became best friends? On this particular subject, objective honesty will get you summarily tossed out of the boat. In a world that puts fourteen-year-olds on the cover of *Vogue*, one's invite into our inner circle is determined simply by your ability to say "You look *fabulous*" like you mean it.)

About halfway through the evening, I looked over and saw a woman staring at me from another table like she recognized me but wasn't sure from where. I gave her a friendly smile, and a few minutes later, she approached our table. I thought she was going to join us, but as I went to grab her a chair, she looked directly at me and said, "Hi. I'm new to the area, and I'm looking for a good place to get my Botox and other cosmetic injectables. You looked like you would know. Any recommendations?"

I LOOKED LIKE I WOULD KNOW?

As my friends choked on their wine in unrestrained merriment and I desperately searched my brain for how this might even be a *shred* of a compliment, I finally sighed—*what the hell?*—and jotted down the number on a napkin. She left, all happy smiles, chatting on her iPhone as she walked out the door, while I debated running after her and asking her to book a two-for-one.

Apparently I'm overdue.

CHAPTER 43

12 Reasons Sex is Better After 50

"In my sex fantasy, nobody ever loves me for my mind."
—Nora Ephron

SEVERAL YEARS AGO, Diane Keaton starred in a romantic comedy called *Baby Boom*.

In one early scene, she and Hubs were sitting in bed together, side by side, both reading, with the bedside clock showing 11 p.m. Diane looks over at Hubs and asks, "Do you want to have sex?"

"Sure," he replies. The next scene shows the two of them exactly like they were earlier, but both wearing smiles; the clock reads 11:03.

This scene cracks me up every time, and I love how it captures middle-age sex. Not because it only took three minutes, which was hilarious (where do we think the word "quickie" came from?), but because they were both smiling and obviously satisfied with their recent adult playdate. One of the best things about middle-age sex is the freedom and confidence to have it the way you want it.

If you're waxing nostalgic about your twenties and thirties, reliving epic prank stories from your college days, sentimental memories of your wedding, and endless tales about raising your uber-amazing offspring, you might also remember personal insecurities, financial struggles, new babies, months of sleep deprivation, and career anxieties (honestly, would you *be* twenty-five again?), none of which lends itself to freestyle sex on demand, despite the enthusiasm and willingness of youth.

But by the time we're in our fifties and beyond, our kids are grown and out the door, our careers are established, we're reasonably financially stable, and life isn't such a struggle. Simply put, we're more relaxed about most things, and sex is often more *fun*.

1. No one expects thongs and thigh-highs under everything you wear. TV starlets are invariably wearing tiny lace bras with matching thongs and thigh-high stockings under everything from yoga pants to suits. Who goes to work like that? If we choose to bust out the lacy dental floss, we can change into it when the time is right. We don't need to be "alert and always prepared" like a trampy Girl Scout at summer camp.

2. We can finally put four-inch stilettos where they belong. In the bedroom. And we're putting them on in bed, because limping to the bedroom, yelling, "Ouch, ouch, ouch!" is not foreplay.

3. We no longer have to invent sudden migraines or imaginary menstrual cramps if we're not in the mood. Some days, we'd rather watch a movie in our one-size-fits-all pink-leopard-print Snuggie (I know you have one), preferably on separate couches. No explanations necessary.

4. We worry less about having a perfect body. Yep, boobs are swaying like palm fronds in a tropical windstorm and cellulite makes our thighs look like five-pound bags of rice, but he hasn't seen the six-pack abs of his youth for at least two decades. Ain't nobody pointing any fingers. So WTH, turn the lights back on and have fun.

5. The journey becomes as important as the destination. 'Nuf said.

6. We can't get pregnant. Let's face it. In our fertile years, no birth control (abstinence excluded) is 100% guaranteed, so that possibility, however slim, hovers over every late-night booty call. There's a fabulous freedom in knowing there's not even the tiniest chance that today's hay romp will result in 427,000 repetitive choruses of *Little Bunny Foo Foo* over the next several years.

7. Nobody has to ask "Was it good for you?" By this age, we can pretty much figure that out without asking. And if you don't know what to look for, you weren't paying attention in your earlier years (which, ironically, pretty much answers the question).

8. We can leave the Kama Sutra to the young. Most of those positions are stupid and/or impossible unless you're both twelve-year-old Romanian gymnasts. Variety can be fun, but pulled hamstrings and strained backs (usually accompanied by shouts of "Get off me, get off me!") tend to kill the mood faster than a drunken phone call from your ex. We recognize our limitations and leave the Indian Headstand to the young. They're bendier, and they heal faster.

9. We can have sex in any room of the house. The kids are gone. As in "not home now, not coming home later, and we've turned his bedroom into a home gym"-type gone. We don't have to lock any doors or stay in the bedroom. If we have neighbors, we may (or may not… you showboats) close the blinds, but other than that, we get to explore the house from a whole different perspective.

10. We learn to work around small distractions. The dog scratching at the door and whining to get in to see what Daddy is doing to Mommy? Don't even hear it. And if Fido somehow manages to get in and tries to stare us down in the act? What the hell. We carry on.

11. We tend to go to bed earlier, which also means earlier sex. After years of youthful and often alcohol-induced "Oh my God, it's 2 a.m., and I've got to work tomorrow" sex, we've discovered that 8 p.m. and sober is great, too. Who knew?

12. We've discovered that laughter during sex can be a good thing. Got a foot cramp? A touch of gastrointestinal distress? Fell off the bed trying something new? Admit it, people. Sex can be *funny*. So unless you're staring at your partner's junk while doubled over in uncontrolled merriment (virtually guaranteeing no sex with that person again, *ever*), spontaneous, joyful laughter can be the most erotic sound in the world.

So, to our children, who think they invented great sex (or any sex, for that matter), and our grandchildren, who will believe the same thing in twenty or so years, carry on with your randy selves. Someday you'll be our age, and then the sex will *really* be great.

CHAPTER 44

30 Things You Might Not Know About Your Wife

"Men will never understand how joyful it makes us feel to unsnap that bra, whip it through our shirtsleeve, and fling it across the room."
—Alex Elle

SINCE THE DAWN OF TIME, men have complained that women are hard to understand. During my lifetime, I've had two dads, three older brothers, and three husbands, and every single one of them claims that women are, essentially, unexplainable. We're secretive and moody, and no matter how hard our men try to truly know us, we remain a mystery.

So, in the spirit of love and sharing, I thought I'd offer my male readers a rare, insider's peek at the female species, with a list of things you might not know about us. You're welcome.

1. 99% of the items in our closet (including those fabulous black boots from Nordstrom) weren't on sale. But they were…, well…, fabulous.

2. We weigh 7 pounds more than we tell you we do. Because if we tell you what we really weigh, you'll think we're fat.

3. We scratch our boobs when we take our bras off at night. At least we have a reason. We're still not sure why you scratch your junk.

4. We think about sex with you. A lot. But by 9 p.m., we're usually too tired to do anything about it. The good news is that if we were going to jump someone's bones, they would be yours.

5. We regularly inspect our bodies, naked, from all angles, checking for anything that jiggles, ripples, or sags. This includes looking over one shoulder and shaking our booties to assess the urgency of getting back to spin class. And you will never see us do this. Ever.

6. We can actually cook. We just don't want to. Believe it or not, not all women come out of the chute holding a spatula and your mom's recipes.

7. We did eat those last four cookies. And *then* blamed the dog. Yep, little Precious has a sweet tooth. We were as surprised as you are.

8. We love you deeply, but, every now and then, we miss the romantic intensity of falling in love. Buy us flowers from time to time. I know we say we don't want you to spend the money. We're lying.

9. Our morning leg shave also includes plucking errant hairs from our nose, toes, chin, lips, and nipples. It takes vigilance to keep our bodies looking like hairless cats. And some things can't be unseen.

10. When we say, "No, I don't want dessert," order the Death-by-Chocolate for yourself. With an extra spoon. And then don't say a word.

11. We tell our best friend pretty much everything. More than you'd like, but less than you think. But we promise never to tell her about that unfortunate unsolicited karaoke attempt in Las Vegas with the Elvis impersonator and your subsequent arrest. At least until your record is expunged.

12. We still love it when you fix our car, carry our bags, or kill the spiders. Chivalry still turns us on.

13. We hold our boobs up when we jog. Our butts already jiggle when we run. We don't need both sides of our bodies flopping at the same time, and we can't hold onto our asses.

14. "No, you don't need to do anything special for my birthday" never means *"No, you don't need to do anything special for my birthday."* Treat me like the once-in-a-lifetime find that I am. You'll like my response.

15. We really don't like Ted, your old college buddy. Frat boys should not be fifty-eight.

16. Yes, we get "work done" on our faces and don't tell you about it. "Hi Babe, I just paid $400 to have botulism injected into my face. And how was your day…?" will never come out of our mouths.

17. Yes, we do actually mind if you have lunch with your newly divorced high school flame. And if she lays her hand on your arm and tosses her hair back one more time, she's going down.

18. We really don't want to hear stories about your ex or any past relationships. We prefer to believe there was no one before us. After all, we were virgins when we met you.

19. Our skin is not naturally this smooth. A lot of work goes into skin that feels like a baby's bottom, and if the bathroom door is locked, you're not getting in.

20. "No, I didn't throw it away. I don't know where it is" is most likely a lie. We did. We do. And it was ugly.

21. Unless it's "You look beautiful" or "You're getting too thin," we never truly want your honest opinion about how we look. Only two responses. Memorize them and we'll both be happy.

22. We settle fights with you in our heads by mentally reenacting the argument when we're alone. And we always win.

23. We like porn. Just not your porn. We didn't buy *Fifty Shades of Grey* (paperback, Kindle, <u>and</u> audio versions) for the fashion tips.

24. When we tell you we're running errands, we're shopping. Duh.

25. When we tell you we're having lunch with a girlfriend, we're shopping. See #24.

26. We get hit on when we're not with you. But we never, ever respond.

27. We often dress more for other women than we do for you. When you say, "Great boots," we hear, "What did you spend?" When she says, "Great boots," we hear, "You look fabulous."

28. We Googled your ex-girlfriends. All of them.

29. Underneath that hot little black dress you love to see us in is a push-up bra, thigh-to-waist Spanx, and the occasional Depends (discreet, of course). Why do you think we get undressed in the bathroom?

30. When we give you a long slow kiss, we're not necessarily saying, "Let's have sex." But we might be. Some mystery is a good thing.

CHAPTER 45

From MILF to Middle-Age.
25 Signs It's Happened to You.

"I always wanted to be somebody, but now I realize I should have been more specific."
—Lily Tomlin

SPENDING MUCH OF MY adult life in retail, I've come to the conclusion that many women don't know when it's time to let go of an era and move gracefully to the next chapter. (And I'm not throwing stones. After viewing the unfortunate photos from last summer's family barbeque, I recently bequeathed a few clothing favorites to my DIL that I apparently should have passed on years ago.)

Let's face it. We all struggle with aging and the inevitable visible signs of the permanent passage of our youth. But ultimately, we need to accept that what's hot when you're twenty can make you look like a cougar at thirty, a MILF at forty, and an aging hooker at fifty.

So to help clear this up for the fifty-plus crowd, here are a few signs that it might be time to consider passing the baton of youth to the next generation of MILFs and start rocking your middle-aged years.

1. You know that look on a man's face when he meets you for the first time and you know he's thinking, "Hmmm... Maybe..."? Yeah, *that* look. You haven't seen that on any guy under seventy since 2009.

2. Your son's friends no longer tell him how hot his mother is. They refer to you as ma'am, and they help carry your groceries, not because they're trying to impress you, but because they're afraid you'll fall and hurt yourself.

3. Your plastic surgeon asks, "Why did you wait so long?" and offers a complimentary lipo procedure with your tummy tuck because, well, he cares about you.

•

4. The twelve-year-old at the cosmetics counter starts recommending expensive creams for those "nasty age spots" and lines around your eyes.

5. Waiters and store clerks no longer ask you for your ID, even as a flirty joke. And if you suggest it, they just look confused.

6. You buy your bras at Bra World rather than Victoria's Secret, with underwires, side panels, and wide straps to hoist those tired Beanie Babies up and out. This is no longer about foreplay. This is war. Us against gravity. Guess who wins?

7. You own at least six different styles of Spanx, including the full-body, suck-in-everything tube girdle, but you rarely wear them because, quite frankly, it's just not that important anymore.

8. Makeup now needs new techniques that often require professional instruction. Skip it altogether, and five decades of questionable lifestyle choices (tanning beds, too much alcohol, too little exercise, bad food choices, stressful careers, and shared parenting with your ex-husband, The Douche, and his twenty-six-year-old wife, Porn Star Barbie) are imprinted on our faces for all the world to see. Simply spackling it on in an attempt to cover signs of aging, like a teenager trying to hide a breakout, can result in foundation falling into our lines, lipstick bleeding into the crevices around our lips, and eyeshadow glittering like a child's school craft project.

9. We still work out, but the parts we used to skip (the warm-up, the cool-down, and the stretching) are now the reason we're there. Yesterday's spinning class is now Tai Chi, often followed by a nap. It's less about achieving peach-pit butts (who are we kidding?) than about being able to bend over far enough to put on our socks without breaking a sweat.

10. Every story you tell about anything that happened before 1990 ends with, "Can you believe that was twenty-five years ago? It seems like yesterday!"

11. Sales clerks stopped asking years ago if you and your adult daughter are sisters and assume any child with you under fifteen is your grandchild.

12. Sex is still great, but you've taken down the trapeze and the stripper pole. When the body parts swing one way and the support structures swing another, it's time to explore new options. Preferably ones that don't require gymnastics-level flexibility, thong underwear, more than one glass of wine, or participation after 10 p.m.

13. People see old photos of you and exclaim, "You look so young here! When was this taken?"

14. You go to your high school reunion and everybody looks so old. Then you realize they're the same age as you.

15. Your online dating profile gets double the hits after you add "Previous senior caregiving" to the Experience field.

16. Any attempt to flirt with the twenty-something hot male checker at the local supermarket makes you look less like a cougar and more like a crazy cat lady.

17. The pretty pink flower you had tattooed right above your left butt cheek has grown with your hips over the years, and now resembles a weird, drooping gladiola painted on your ass.

18. Your Kegel exercises are less about improving your sex life and more about controlling bladder leakage every time you laugh.

19. Your metabolism has slowed to the point where you have to choose between wine and carbohydrates to avoid looking like a pufferfish. You haven't had a bagel in two years.

20. When your man asks you for a "back rub," that's really all he wants.

21. When you lament the passage of your youth, you're talking about your forties.

22. Dinner with another couple is spent talking about bodily ailments, upcoming surgeries, grandkids, and retirement plans. And you're all home by nine.

23. For your anniversary, Hubs gives you a day at the spa, which essentially means you're spending the day alone. And you're thrilled.

24. Your kids turn fifty. 'Nuf said.

Last weekend, Hubs and I were sitting with a group of friends at a local winery, swapping raucous stories about misspent youth and the hilarious hardships of aging. As one entertaining older gentleman was recounting a lively, detailed tale about getting older in a society that worships youth, sending all of us into fits of laughter, he looked over at me with a broad smile and shouted over the crowd, "Well, *you* know what I mean, right?!"

And there's my sign.

CHAPTER 46

What Doesn't Kill You Makes You Thinner

"I've gained and lost the same 10 pounds so many times, my cellulite has déjà vu."
—Jane Wagner

I LOVE HOLLYWOOD. It's fun, silly, and just weird enough to make me feel normal. A recent issue of *Star Magazine* (yes, I subscribe... Don't judge) featured an anorexic child actress extolling the virtues of a new diet pill, saying it "gave her back her figure." (Back from where? In your sixteen genetically-blessed-and-never-had-a-baby years on this planet, what? Were you up, like, eight ounces this morning?)

This got me thinking about my weight battle over the years. When your sister is a size two and your mother is a size six, a size eight to ten makes you the chubby one. My youth is littered with remnants of stupid diet tricks that scream "What was I *thinking*?"

Here's where you ask, "So what did you do?"

Okay, here goes. My personal "Yep, I really did" diet confessions:

In my twenties:

1. Smoking. My ninety-two-pound college roommate assured me that if I smoked when I got hungry, I'd lose weight. Six months later, I was a chubby smoker. Yeah, *that* got me dates.

2. Laxatives. Great idea if you plan to live your life locked in your bathroom. And even if you *could* come out long enough to go anywhere, every dating conversation will be interrupted with promises to "Be right back!" as you scramble for the nearest ladies room at sixty-second intervals. (On one particularly promising evening, by the fourth time I came back, he'd gone home. Ended the date and the diet.)

3. Purging. A fancy word for "making yourself throw up." (Hey, it was good enough for Princess Diana.) Still, the thought of sticking my finger down my throat to make myself throw up pretty much made me, well… throw up. Moving on.

In my thirties:

4. The Martini Diet. Second cousin to the Smoking Diet, but with gin. Since I don't *like* gin, I substituted Kahlua and cream. Gained four pounds in the first week.

5. The Tapeworm Diet. Okay, I didn't actually try this one. But I *thought about it*. A tiny little guy that lives in your tummy and eats all the junk you ingest before it hits your hips? That's a better fairy tale than *Snow White*. Alas, since I couldn't find a store that actually sold tapeworms, it was not to be.

6. The Phen/Fen Diet. Basically, this stuff is Chinese speed. Didn't lose any weight, but damn, I got shit *done*. By the third consecutive night of *no sleep*, I looked like crap and face-planted into my fettuccine at Ye Old Spaghetti House, snoring into my cream sauce until Hubs carried me out, shouting out to the patrons something about "bad shrimp."

In my forties:

7. The Praise the Lord Diet. This program tells you that God *wants* you to be hungry, as a sign of humility and gratitude. By day five, I was decidedly *ungrateful* and quit going to church. (I eventually went back because they were having their annual potluck after the service. God and I made up over homemade mac 'n' cheese, and He told me He never authorized a diet book. Ha! I knew it.)

8. The Cookie Diet. These are large "cookies" made up of oats, bran, fiber, and sawdust. They taste like drywall and are intended to replace food you actually *like*. You can't drink enough water (okay, wine) to swallow these, so I substituted two boxes of Girl Scout Thin Mints. The next morning's weigh-in suggested that "Eat Cookies and Lose Weight!" was a bit misleading.

9. Fasting. This worked until I got… how can I put this… oh yeah, *hungry*. The world's only three-hour diet. Whose *idiot idea* was this? If I had the willpower to *not eat*, the aforementioned Dumb Ideas #1-8 would have been limited to The Wine Lover's Diet. (No, you won't lose an ounce, but you won't care!)

And now, in my fifties:

10. The Screw It, I Feel Great Diet. Ooh, is that a brownie?

CHAPTER 47

Those are *Real*? Apparently God Takes Visa

"I'm in the public eye, so I don't care who knows what I get done. If I see something sagging, dragging, or bagging, I get it sucked, tucked, or plucked."
—Dolly Parton

A FRIEND OF MINE recently had her breasts "upsized," and she's determined that no one will ever know they're not natural. Okay, babe. Love ya, but we need a tiny reality check here. You're fifty. You weigh 103 pounds, and you're a size two. (*And* we're still friends, which shows what a secure woman I am. *snort-laugh* But you're hysterically funny, so I overlook my middle-age body envy and love you anyway.) They're a full, bosomy D-cup, *and* the good doc placed them up around your clavicles. Repeat after me: *No one* is going to believe they're real.

Having spent several years in beauty retail, I've concluded that cosmetic surgery is the final taboo. As a society that shares (OMG, do we *share*) every minute detail of our personal lives on Facebook and Twitter, we are nevertheless inexplicably reluctant to admit to having "work done." We freely admit to dropping out of college to join a cult in Idaho for two years, to recently finishing our fourth stint in rehab, or coming out of the closet this year after two marriages and three kids. We unabashedly post the entire saga on Facebook, sharing all the juicy details with a few thousand virtual friends. But Botox? *That* stays firmly tucked away on a tiny appointment card, securely stashed in our wallets where even our best friends will never see it.

Personally, I think you should do whatever the hell you want and can afford (unless you're Cat Woman. For the love of God, somebody *stop her*). But please stop trying to pretend that your perky, perfectly symmetrical, fifty-four-year-old breasts are *natural*. I call this "God loves me more than He loves you" syndrome. Why else would God give you those gravity-defying orbs and stick *me* with two beagle ears on a stick? That's just *mean*. And since the Bible repeatedly tells us God is a loving deity, I have to assume you intervened and gave the Big Guy a little creative assistance.

For those of you who occasionally look at a woman and wonder, here are a couple of quick, telltale signs:

- ❖ If her forehead is smooth as a baby's bottom and *doesn't move* when she's talking, she's a Botox'er.
- ❖ If she has a perfectly flat belly after three kids and her idea of exercise is opening a second bottle of wine, she's been hoovered by a lipo-vac.
- ❖ If she's a size zero, but has perfect, size-D breasts that don't fall to the side when she's sunbathing, those puppies were a birthday gift from someone other than the Good Lord.

In short, if you look like an upside-down Weeble, with zero percent body fat except for two large melons stuck to your chest, give it up. Not even your preschool grandchildren are buying the "natural" argument. Stop pretending you were divinely chosen to be prettier, thinner, or younger-looking than the rest of us born in your decade. If you've had it nipped, tucked, sucked, injected, lifted, or enhanced, consider sharing *that* if we ask. Even if we choose a different path, our self-esteem will remain intact knowing that we didn't somehow draw the beauty short straw.

And lest you think I'm holding out, I'll go first. When I hit fifty, I had an upper and lower blepharoplasty. In short, an "eye job." For years I was unhappy with the drooping of my upper eyelids and the constant puffiness underneath that no amount of expensive eye creams would deflate.

Admittedly, there *was* a tiny part of me that hoped the doc would take one look at me and announce, "*You*? You look great. Come back in a few years." That faint hope went south on a luge when he peered over at me and said, "Are you *sure* you don't want a full forehead lift? We could get a lot more of that sagging." Awesome.

"Nope," I replied. "I'm not going for 'stunned.' Just more rested. Eyes only, doc."

In hindsight, I probably should've read the fine print under "Healing." Specifically, how *long* it takes. When doc said I'd be able to wear makeup and go out within a week or so, he *didn*'t say I would still look like I'd gone head first through a car windshield. (I attended a friend's wedding shortly after the surgery wearing giant, oversize black sunglasses, feeling all Audrey Hepburn. Later photos revealed a stronger resemblance to Snookie. Epic vanity fail.)

But, several weeks later, when all was finally over and healed, I looked, well… *rested*. I loved it.

Would I do it again? Absolutely. And if you ever ask, I'll give you the name of my doctor.

·

CHAPTER 48

They Say Beauty is in the Eye of the Beholder.
But Photoshop Can't Hurt.

"Even I don't wake up looking like Cindy Crawford."
—Cindy Crawford

WHEN HUBS AND I were approaching our fifth wedding anniversary, he announced that he wanted to renew our vows. "It's too soon," I explained. "Nobody thinks five years is really a *landmark*."

"It is to *me*," he replied. "I've been married twice before, and both marriages went belly up at the end of the fourth year. So to still be happily married at this point is a record for me!"

Notwithstanding the validity of that statement and the fact that it wasn't exactly a ringing endorsement of marital fortitude, I silently agreed that something celebratory was called for. So I decided to have some fun photos taken. Since Hubs loves all things retro and vintagey, I thought he'd like a series of pin-up, 1940s-style cheesecake pics. More Rita Hayworth/Jayne Mansfield, less Playboy porn star. (I was *fifty*, after all.)

I wasn't comfortable calling up the nearest local photographer (I could hear him laughing as he asked, "You want me to make you look like *what*?"), so I called one of my best girlfriends, who's a fabulous amateur photographer, and she immediately offered to help.

A few quick calls to some girlfriends resulted in an astonishing array of costume changes that made me feel like Cher at the Forum. (Apparently, vintage cheesecake has a surprisingly mass appeal to the male over-fifty set. Who knew?)

Next, we Googled "WWII pin-up photos" to find poses that we thought I could pull off. We waited a few days until Hubs was out on a construction project (working with girlfriend's husband, who was instructed to call us *immediately* if Hubs left the job site). Then, with costumes in place and Google shots on the kitchen counter, we got together at my house for the shoot.

As I lay on the floor on my back, legs straight up and arms overhead (classic cheesecake pose), girlfriend instructed me to "look sexy." All attempts for me to say "Come hither" with my eyes resulted in her dissolving into unrestrained merriment, choking out, "You look like you need to pee. Try *again!*" Two hours and a bottle of wine later, it was obvious that I was singularly lacking in "bedroom eyes," but we carried on.

Somewhat later, we got the obviously wine-induced bright idea to use Hubs's Harley as a prop. The only problem was that his Harley was in our overcrowded, gray garage. Although girlfriend had a Photoshop program to soften the backgrounds, remove shadows, and even provide a little technological nip/tuck to my shape, there were limits to what it could do. Photoshop wasn't going to help the garage. We needed to move the bike. *Into the house.*

Desperately hoping the neighbors weren't home, I backed my car out of the garage to get to Hubs's bike and dashed back into the house, wearing nothing but a military-style jacket, fishnets, and high heels, while girlfriend rolled the motorcycle into the living room and down the hall towards the bedroom (thank God for hardwood floors), where the other pictures were taken. She pushed the back and I steered the front until Hubs's beloved Harley Low-Rider was snuggly parked in the master bedroom.

Two costume changes (and another bottle of wine) later, we were having a ball. Then the phone rang.

"He's on his way," our outlook reported. "ETA, twenty minutes."

OMG! As I scrambled back into my yoga pants and shoved all the evidence under the bed, girlfriend turned the Harley around and started to roll it out the door, where it got stuck. As in *wedged into* the angled doorway. As in NOT MOVING. ("Hi, honey. How was your day? And by the way, your Harley is stuck in the bedroom door frame. Don't ask.")

Watching the clock, we frantically pushed and pulled, pushed and pulled, until it shot forward like a champagne cork; we wheeled it into the garage just as Hubs' truck pulled into the driveway.

Two weeks later, girlfriend brought over the "improved" proofs. They were *fabulous*. My legs were longer, my tummy was flatter, and my boobs were back up where the Good Lord had intended them to be. My only concern was that he'd take one look and ask, "Who *is* this?" But I proudly presented him with the framed photos on our anniversary. He loved them, insisting, despite all evidence to the contrary, that the woman in the photos did bear some resemblance to his wife. He shows them to more people than I'm quite comfortable with, but at least I'm not in a bikini. Yeah, *that* would be embarrassing.

Then a family member saw them a few weeks later, took a long look, and announced, "Wow, someone Photoshopped the *crap* out of these, eh?"

Well, ouch.

What the hell. Years from now, when I'm dead and gone, my grandchildren will find these and say, "Grandma was *hot*."

CHAPTER 49

The Insider's Guide to Makeup Products.
Where to Save, Where to Splurge.

"The most beautiful makeup for a woman is passion. But cosmetics are easier to buy."
—Yves Saint Laurent

I GOT A CALL FROM a girlfriend recently, all breathless and excited, having just seen an ad for a mascara that promised to "make my eyelashes look like falsies. But it's $35," she wailed. "Should I try it?"

Friends know that I've been in the beauty industry for, well... *ever*, and I'm an unabashed beauty-product junkie. I love the colors, the textures, the rich tubes, and the promises... Oh, the promises: of thicker lashes, fuller pouts, and youthful blush, no matter how not-twenty-something we might be.

After a quick response to her question (No, you do not need to spend $35 on your mascara), she suggested I write a chapter on where to splurge and where to save on makeup products. I love it when friends and family suggest essay ideas (helps avoid nasty writer's block)!

Assuming you're on a good-quality skin care routine, makeup can even out your skin tone, make the eyes look bigger and brighter, put some youthful blush in your cheeks, and sexy up those pouty lips. Makeup can make good skin glow.

But, like anything else, makeup products vary widely in quality and price. So here are a few insider tips into where to save and where to splurge.

1. Brushes. We have to start here, because the quality of your brushes makes a *huge* difference in the quality of your makeup application. A good brush makes an inexpensive product look smoother, whereas a cheap brush can make a Chanel blusher streaky. Drugstore brushes are like painting your house with a whisk broom. They pick up and lay down color unevenly, they make blending difficult, and they often start shedding quickly. Buy good ones. You don't need a lot. A fat, fluffy, all-over brush for powder or bronzer, a blusher brush, and a couple of eyeshadow brushes should do it. But go to Nordstrom or Sephora and get the best you can afford. Your makeup will look better, they feel yummy on your skin, and they'll last you for years.

2. Foundation. Get out of the drugstores. Most drugstore foundations have a lot of pink in them (weird, since most skin tones are yellow-based), which can look chalky. And since most drugstores don't have testers, you can burn through a whack of money trying to pin down the right color. Cheaper foundations also tend to be heavier, with uneven consistency, making them harder to blend. Foundation is supposed to look like great skin. Higher-quality foundations are sheerer, easier to blend, can be perfectly color-matched by a skilled makeup artist, and often contain marvelous things like light reflectors that give the skin a luminous (think "younger") look.

3. Blusher. This is a product where you can go in whatever direction you want. If your brush is good, the drugstore brands are fine. Department store prices are largely about the upscale compact the product comes in. If you're a fan of shimmer, try to avoid the super-cheap ones that look like they've been infused with glitter. Shimmer and glitter are *not* interchangeable, especially if you're over fifty. Shimmer is subtle and pretty. Glitter is for six-year-old fairy princesses and prepubescent figure skaters from *Disney on Ice*.

4. Eyeshadow. This depends upon your ability to blend. Drugstore eyeshadow tends to be heavier and more pigmented than department-store versions, which can look harsh or overly done if not extremely well blended. But drugstore brands can be a reasonably safe bet if you use a high-quality brush, stick with neutral colors, and be cautious about the sparkles (see **Blusher**, above). If you're hopping on the colored-eyeshadow trend this year, seriously consider moving up. Cheaper blue eyeshadows can be brighter and more truck stop waitress than the heathered hues of Estee Lauder. Leave the $4 Crayola colors to the tweeners.

5. Mascara. This is a tough one, because the only thing more subjective than fragrance is mascara. Every woman has her favorite, and God help any makeup artist who tries to take it away from her. The good news is that there's no reason to spend extra money on this one. The current "battle of the wands," with each brand claiming that their wand is somehow magic because it's curved or fatter or longer, is just stupid. Some of the most prominent beauty-industry powerhouses I know have used Maybelline for decades and will never switch. My personal favorites? L'Oréal Voluminous for day and Rimmel Outrageous Retro Glam whenever I want lashes out to *there*. Both available at Walmart.

6. **Lipstick**. Like blushers, drugstore and upscale department store lipsticks have very little difference in the product itself. The consistency and the color options are similar. The primary difference is in the containers. Department store brands often come in gorgeous, expensive-looking gold or silver tubes that "click" when you close them, making you feel glamorous whenever you pull them out of your purse. They're like fabulous Prada sunglasses versus knock-offs from the Eyeglass Barn at the outlet mall. Drugstore brands are usually in plastic tubes that just say, "Git 'er done." But either way, they look the same on your lips. Your call on this one.

7. **Pressed Powder/Bronzer**. Like foundations, it's very difficult to find cheaper versions of these products that look like real skin. The cheap ones are heavier, harder to blend, and often come in un-skintone-friendly shades (especially bronzers, which all seem to be made at the Oompa-Loompa factory). They tend to quickly migrate into fine lines, making them more visible. Better brands come in real-women colors. They're also more finely milled, don't settle into lines, and contain light reflectors that give the skin a gorgeous, soft matte finish that their drugstore counterparts can't match.

8. **Eye/Lip Pencil**. Suffice it to say that there are only a few places, worldwide, that manufacture makeup pencils. The part of the product that you apply is simply encased and labeled uniquely for every brand. (Do you see where this is going?) Pick these up anywhere.

My best advice? Go to a local department store or Sephora, find a salesperson whose look you like (preferably in your same age decade) and ask for help. Makeup at fifty-plus is very different than makeup for the twenty-something set. An hour of professional advice can be the smartest decision you can make.

CHAPTER 50

Aging Gracefully. Not as Easy as it Sounds.

"The hardest years in life are those between ten and seventy."
—Helen Hayes

I RECENTLY OVERHEARD a conversation between two gorgeous twenty-somethings, all toned bodies, porcelain skin, perfect teeth, mile-high legs, butts you could bounce a quarter off of, and boobs still up where God originally put them. One held up her wine glass, making a toast, and declared, "I don't believe in plastic surgery. I'm going to age *naturally*." Her friend nodded, and as they clinked glasses, she declared with a self-satisfied smile, "Me, too. I'm never getting anything 'done.' Those women are pathetic and self-absorbed."

First of all, ouch. Secondly, you're *twelve*. Talk to me in thirty years. You have no credibility on this subject, so shut up.

But before I get blasted for being anti-aging, this chapter comes after an earlier one that listed my *Top 10 Best Things About Aging*.

But there's nothing inherently graceful about aging in a society that dismisses the elderly and worships youth. Fifty is called a "senior citizen" in most restaurants, and quite frankly, if we die any time after age fifty, our kids would likely say, "Well, she lived a long life."

There's nothing graceful about breasts gravitating towards our navel, necessitating trading in our lacy, Victoria's Secret "Come here, Big Guy" fantasy bra for a utilitarian cotton sports bra that shoves them back up to our rib cage and holds them tight so they won't smack anybody in a sudden wind storm.

There's nothing graceful about underarm twaddle that rules out anything sleeveless unless we're prepared to keep our arms pinned to our sides all day long. I get exhausted just trying to remember that my triceps are forever banned from public viewing, and I'm considering keeping a burka in the trunk of my car for days I inadvertently leave the house in a tank top.

There's definitely nothing graceful about menopause that requires daily sheet changes because we sweat the equivalent of a kiddie pool every night in our sleep, or sticking our head out of the car window, hair blowing backwards and bugs in our teeth like a border collie in a wind tunnel because *it's too freakin' hot in here.*

There's nothing graceful about gaining ten-plus pounds in your sleep because your metabolism changed overnight and forgot to warn you, often resulting in the bathroom scale being tossed out the nearest open window, followed by a pity party that would make a three-year-old jealous.

Middle age brings with it a plethora of wonderful, Zen-like qualities like serenity, patience, a better sense of humor (which God had the foresight to know we'd need), along with new priorities and adventures. However, it also lets in the shape shifters. Those invisible little seam-busters that quietly, but seemingly overnight, shift your proportions into a body shape you didn't have yesterday.

Even if you've managed to avoid the seemingly obligatory, menopausal ten-pound weight gain, you may arise one morning and discover that *nothing fits.* Dresses you wore yesterday, today you can't zip up. Jeans you rocked for years now make you look like your favorite banana nut muffins from the local deli. Skinny jeans are out because they look like sausage casing on a Ball Park frank. WTH?

The morning I realized I'd been shape-shifted, I was standing in my walk-in closet wailing like the local Krispy Kreme shop had closed its doors, and Hubs came running down the hall, assuming some tragedy had befallen me and I clearly needed his manly-manness to fix it.

"*Are you okay?*" he shouted as he got closer.

"I'm fine," I sniffled, "but I can't wear these clothes. They're all a size eight."

"But don't you wear an eight?" he asked, looking confused in the absence of blood or anything requiring masculine intervention.

"Apparently not anymore," I cried.

"Well, why don't you just buy tens?" Then he grinned, obviously believing he'd just uncovered the magic solution to my visible distress.

"Fine," I replied. "You can take all these clothes to the Salvation Army, while I go to Nordstrom and replace them."

"Holy crap," he stated. "*All of them?*"

Hubs quickly changed the subject and, in a gallant attempt to cheer me up, suggested we go out to dinner. Clinging to my last vestige of self-esteem, I picked out his favorite dress, but as I stepped into it, I knew instinctively that it wasn't going to work. It made it slightly past my knees then stopped. It wasn't going an inch further over my thighs and hips. *Are you kidding me?*

I managed to kick it with enough velocity to send it sailing across the hall just as I burst into tears. Hubs walked up behind me, reached around to my front, and whispered, "I just love your little Buddha belly," as he rubbed it like he was expecting a genie to fly out and grant him a wish.

Tell me he did not just call any part of my body "Buddha."

I responded with a tight smile, because I'm reasonably certain he meant that to be a compliment, but my brain was screaming *May your camel get fleas then sleep in your tent.*

And so I'm learning that aging gracefully is largely about *acceptance.* Exercise and cosmetic intervention will slow down the physical signs of time passing, but in the end, this journey is largely emotional. Part of the process is learning how to be less judgmental and kinder to the people we love.

I'm learning that that includes me.

CHAPTER 51

What Women Love About Marriage

"All you need is love. But a little chocolate now and then doesn't hurt."
—Charles Schultz

A FEW MONTHS AGO, I was thrilled to have an article of mine reprinted on a wildly popular blog. It was called "24 Things Women Want in a Pre-Nup"—Chapter 39 in this book—and I'd originally written it as a lighthearted list of things men do that drive their wives crazy. It had started as a compilation of hilarious comments taken from a boisterous and merry group poll over two pitchers of margaritas at the local cantina; the suggestions were from a diverse group of girlfriends who, like me, are all happily married.

This was also my first post to get trolled.

For my non-blogging readers, "trolls" are people who post mean-spirited, inflammatory comments (often simply a character assassination of the writer) on a blog, deliberately intending to provoke an emotional, online debate. Basically, my trolls said I was a "whiny bitch" (maybe true), in serious need of psychological help (probably true), who hated marriage (absolutely *not* true).

Experienced bloggers tend to agree that the best way to handle trolls is to ignore them, so I didn't respond. But it got me thinking about what I loved most about being married, so I began a new list. A second shout-out to girlfriends for their contributions led to immediate, enthusiastic responses. Here's what makes us happy:

1. He makes me laugh. Every day.

2. I get to sleep every night with my best friend.

3. We're past that awkward first-time sex. No guessing required.

4. I don't have to date anymore.

5. **Kisses.** Lots of kisses.

6. **Someone misses me when I'm gone.**

7. **I always have a plus-one.**

8. **I have someone on my side, even when I'm wrong.**

9. **Every fight doesn't make me wonder if he's changed his Facebook status.**

10. **I'm loved.**

11. **We can have sex anytime we want.** (And if the kids are gone, *anywhere* you want.)

12. **He knows exactly how I like my steak.** And my coffee.

13. **We can have entire conversations without actually speaking.** A look or a touch can say more than words.

14. **I can go out with the girls without having to deal with bad pick-up lines from strangers looking for one-nighters.** "No thanks, I'm married" is the best douche-repellant ever.

15. **I can be silly.** Often.

16. **I can be selfish.** Occasionally.

17. **He's a great snuggle-buddy after a bad dream.**

18. **He ages with me.**

19. **He holds my hand when I'm getting a scary diagnosis.** And doesn't let go.

20. **He shares the joys and worries of parenting.**

21. **He's seen my crazy.** And he's still here.

22. **I no longer have to explain my family members.** He knows all the key players and where all the bodies are buried.

23. **I don't have to know it all.** (I proofread all his emails. He keeps me posted on world events.)

24. **I don't have to do it all.** (He cooks, I clean.)

25. **I don't have to dress "Do Me" all the time.**

26. **He doesn't say a word when I've been avoiding carbs for a month then toss a box of doughnuts and two frozen pizzas in the shopping cart at Safeway.**

27. **He's my best cheerleader when I need encouragement to keep going or applause at the finish line.**

28. **He's a great dragon-slayer when I'm hurt.**

29. **He gets me, even when the rest of the world doesn't.**

30. **He understands my love of cold cereal for dinner and Pop Tarts in my glove box.**

31. He tells me I'm beautiful. Even after an ugly cry.
32. I always have someone to play with.
33. He knows me and loves me anyway.

On a recent evening, Hubs and I were sitting out on the deck, sharing a fabulous bottle of Cabernet and quietly enjoying the warm sunset together. Hubs looked over at me and said, "I'm so lucky to be married to you. But sometimes I think you're too classy for me."

My mind did a quick replay of the energetic, epic fails I've subjected him to over the last fifteen years, and I burst out laughing, knocking over my full glass of wine. The red liquid arced up into the air then splattered squarely down the center of my white T-shirt.

Hubs got up to get me another glass (and a clean T-shirt) and grinned, "Then again, I think we're good."

It doesn't get any better than that.

CHAPTER 52

Becoming a Better Person. This Might Take a While

*"If you have to ask if it's too early to drink wine, you're an amateur and we
can't be friends."*
—Unknown

LIKE MOST PEOPLE, I find myself occasionally taking stock of
myself and my life, looking for things I could do better. To become a
kinder, healthier, stronger, more financially stable, better educated,
more loving wife, mother, and daughter. *Whew.*

Big job. *Big.*

Friends and family can (and often do) cheerfully point out that
the majority of my self-improvement projects quickly torpedo into
blog posts that chronicle my lack of success over the years to be the
"best me I can be."

Recently, I attended a workshop about "finding your inner
Gandhi" or some Zen-like thing, and they had us write down our
personal-improvement challenges in an effort to uncover the reasons
we might be resistant to positive change. We were instructed to list
our top dozen, and were given thirty minutes. I was done in ten. (I'm
nothing if not self-aware.)

My Top 12 Self-Improvement Fails:

1. Eat more vegetables. "More" is misleading. It suggests I eat
any. Never have. Never will. I hate all things green. For years, Mom
would bargain, "If you eat your broccoli, you can have a cookie."
What I heard was, "If you eat that nasty leafy thing, I'll give you
something *wonderful*." After I moved out at eighteen, I said, "Screw
that. I'm going straight for the cookie."

2. Work out daily. I'd love to. Workouts make me feel good. All
those endorphins humming through your body. But I get up at 4

a.m. during the week to write before work from 8 'til 5, then I write in the evenings and on weekends. Precious downtime is spent with Hubs over the barbeque, friends around the table and the wine poured. Fitness fanatics love to sniff, "We all have twenty-four hours in a day. It must not be a *priority* for you." You're right. Toned thighs are less important to me than family, friends, writing, or the job that pays my bills. I promise not to wear a bikini.

3. Say only nice things about other people. I *try* with this one. Really, I do. But the world is just too full of idiots to resist. We've got Boo Boos and Kardashians on the national news, mega-rich divorcing celebrities fighting over the family dog but shipping their kids off to boarding school, stupid criminals who stop to take showers at the home they just burgled, teenage pop stars with million-dollar homes and Serenity Lane on speed dial, superstar athletes who attempt to board planes with loaded weapons in their carry-ons, and on it goes. Some days you just want to shout, "WTF is *wrong* with you people?" They say God isn't dead... Just disappointed. Amen.

4. Save money every month. One of my favorite eCards says, *I don't want to spend money. But I want to buy stuff.* 'Nuf said.

5. Take more care with my weekend appearance. Hubs has remarked (more than once... ouch) that I leave for work every morning looking all "done and fabulous," but when I'm home with him, he gets yoga pants, Walmart T-shirts, and no makeup. Valid point. But all *he* has to do every morning is brush his teeth, rub wet fingers through his hair, slip on jeans and a T-shirt, and he's out the door. Weekends are my break from the two-hour process of getting "done and fabulous." I just tell him that, at fifty-eight, five days on/two days off is a gift. You're welcome.

6. Stop swearing. Yes, I know I should stop cursing. It's not feminine, and it can be offensive (although not to anyone in my social tribe; apparently we were all raised by truck-stop waitresses and drunk sailors). But sometimes an emotion just can't be expressed any other way. A prim "I'm so pleased" just doesn't resonate like a big smile and an "I'm all giddy and shit." I'll work on it.

7. Accept the things I cannot change. This is a tough one for Type A, controlling personalities. We tend to think that if you try hard enough, for long enough, you can fix anything. This may be true if you're talking about a bicycle. But when you're talking about a human, you might as well be trying to teach a fish to sprint. We can't "fix" anyone else. We either love them or we don't, *exactly the way they are.*

8. Face my fears. By fifty-plus, they're called "instincts." I instinctively know that my avoidance of skydiving and bungee jumping is probably healthy and that *not* going downstairs when I hear a loud thud or a crash in the kitchen at 2 a.m. to "see what it is" is not necessarily the wrong decision.

9. Spend less time on Facebook, Twitter, and Pinterest, and more time in the real world. I *want* to. Really, I do. But all my cool friends live in Facebook-land, so I go and hang out with them whenever I can. God, I'm pathetic.

10. Learn moderation. Not. Gonna. Happen. I'm just not a moderation kind of woman. Moderation is for wussies with no *passion* for what they're doing. I never want a headstone that says, *Here Lies Vikki. She Lived Her Life in Moderation. She Was Also the Most Boring Person on the Planet.* I've instructed Hubs to inscribe, *Here Lies Vikki. She Was Crazy, But Damn, She Was FUN.*

11. Be less judgmental about myself. Be kinder, less critical to me. I'm learning that with most things in life, it's okay to fail. It's only not okay to quit trying. (See Chapter 37, *Today I Fired my BFF.* Clearly, I'm a work in progress on this one.)

12. Give up wine. A friend who's lived through every detail of my diet struggles over the years suggested that if I quit drinking wine, I'd cut out a butt-load (pun intended) of empty calories and probably knock off those last ten pounds I've been fighting since 1982. I pondered this for a moment, and I could only respond, *"BAHAHAHAHA!!!"*

My beloved Cabernet *understands* me.

•

CHAPTER 53

Lessons I've Learned From My Middle-Age Body

"If I had to live my life again, I'd make the same mistakes. Only sooner."
—Tallulah Bankhead

LAST MONTH, I TURNED FIFTY-EIGHT. As in "years old." Fifty. Eight.

I don't care who you are, fifty-eight is no longer "young." Body parts have shifted downwards. Skin has lost its memory yarn. Thighs ripple when we're standing still. Once-defined triceps now flap like sheets on a clothesline. Weight has moved into our hips and bellies with the tenacity of squatters on the back forty of the Ponderosa.

But today, I got to thinking about the *beauty* of aging. Yes, I'm aware that my boobs are no longer up around my clavicles (frankly, they haven't been within Howdy-neighbor proximity for several years), but honestly, would you *be* twenty-three again? All perky boobs and flawless skin but often in exchange for angst and uncertainty? Middle age brings with it a certain peace about ourselves and our bodies that is ultimately *liberating*.

So, for my birthday, to balance the scales of the eight billion articles and blog posts (including my own) about the *"seriously?"* side of menopause and the sudden tsunami of AARP applications in our mailbox, I decided to write about the 10 Best Lessons I've Learned from my Middle-Age Body.

1. Humility. I've come to realize that there are certain things I can't control. While it's true that we can go to the gym, watch what we eat, and otherwise stop beating the crap out of our temples, and we can even choose to refresh God's handiwork with a little nip/tuck along the way, the fact remains that *we cannot stop the aging process.* In a society that worships youth and firm thighs, it is no longer *our* *turn*. Let it go, and let the next generation have their day. They will be us someday.

2. Compassion. I'm less judgmental. About myself and about other women in my age bracket. If I have a second piece of cheesecake, I'm not a weak, pathetic behemoth who'll be fat forever because she has absolutely no self-discipline. And if I see another women who's overweight (by today's ridiculous standards), I don't automatically conclude that she's a sloth who just needs to put down the damn fork. Maybe she's genetically curvy and has other, higher priorities than the exhausting pursuit of flat abs at age sixty. I like her already.

3. The importance of a sense of humor. If we haven't learned to laugh at ourselves by now, we need to take a class. It's time to find the funny in this whole process. (God knows, we have enough material.) Otherwise, we eventually start looking like that Cat Woman (or half of Hollywood), with too many surgeries and too many diets that end up making us look creepy and desperate. I'd rather my kids say, "She was a hilarious old broad when she died" than, "We lost Mom on her last face lift, but our children no longer have nightmares."

4. Patience. When you're young, if you want to lose five pounds by Saturday, you can start on Thursday and hit your goal. By fifty-plus, five pounds can be a month's work. And if your last workout was in 2010, you're a good six months away from firm thighs. But I've decided that's okay, and I'm resetting my bar.

5. Exercise should be fun. It's like sex. If you're not having a good time, you're doing it wrong. Do what you like. You'll do it more often and get better results. (True on both counts.)

6. Comparisons are pointless. There will always be somebody thinner, prettier, and younger than you. And if you look for it, you can always find someone fatter, homelier, and older than you. *Who cares?* When I meet the woman who cures cancer, *then* I'll be intimidated.

7. Listen to my body. I've stopped trying to tell it what it needs, what's it supposed to be doing, and what it should look like. If it says I'm tired, I take a nap. If it feels stiff, I do some stretching. If it craves something sweet, I have a cookie (okay, four... don't judge. See #2). My body is no longer the enemy, needing to be beaten into submission for daily infractions of not being tall enough, pretty enough, or thin enough. It is what it is, and now it tells *me* what to do.

8. When God taketh away, He giveth something better. When we stop mourning the loss of smooth skin, Learjet-level metabolism, and any body parts that could be even loosely described as "perky," we discover an increased sex drive, the end of periods or pregnancy scares, more confidence, and less anxious self-absorption about how we look, leaving us free to reinvent ourselves in whatever way we choose. I'm thinking we came out ahead on this deal.

9. If Hubs buys me something sexy, I wear it. Even if I think I'm too old, too fat, too soft, too... just too fifty-eight. I've learned that how *he* sees me and how *I* see me are vastly different. He doesn't want a twenty-year-old beach volleyball player. He wants *me*. So I dim the lights and strut my stuff, in all its goofy, middle-aged glory.

10. Time will always win. 'Nuf said.

So my advice for the middle-age blahs? Grab your iPod, find your best boogie song, turn it up *LOUD*, and do your naked happy dance in the bathroom mirror. Bust all your worst moves (the ones that make your kids want to move to another state and disclaim all relation to you). All those body parts a-flying and butts jiggling are guaranteed to get you laughing and put the yippy back in your skippy.

Try it. You know you want to. We'll wait.

MORE RAVES

"Vikki's stories always have me either laughing out loud or smiling to myself in a knowing manner."
~ Alexandra Williams, MA *FunAndFit.org*

"In a world where we are often subjected to torturously boring tomes written by our peers, it's awfully nice to find a lighthearted book that doesn't compromise authenticity for entertainment's sake."
~ Alicia Searcy, *Spashionista.com*

"If I am having a bad day, I read a chapter or two and the laugh therapy keeps me going."
~ Lynne Cobb, *lynnecobb.com*

"Witty, self-deprecating and wise, this is the girlfriend you want to sit down and share a couple glasses bottles of wine with."
~ Roxanne Jones, *boomerhaiku.com*

"After reading this hilarious tribute to women of the midlife tribe, I've applied for my "Big Girl Panties Society" membership card and hope to soon learn the secret handshake at the next meeting."
~ Kimberly Dalferes, Author, *Magic Fishing Panties*

"Told with warmth, humor and a twisted take on real life, my only disappointment is that this funny lady is not my neighbor."
~ Kimberly Montgomery, *fiftyjewels.com*

"Vikki has the capacity to create word pictures so vivid they allow you to see her traumatizing her son, wriggling into Spanx and having her dress eaten by a vacuum cleaner."
~ Anne Penniston Gray, BA, BSW, MSW, RSW (SK)

"She is honest about aging, without being negative. She is sarcastically witty about her marriage, without being mean. She pokes fun at herself, and some gruesomely embarrassing mistakes she makes, without being self-deprecating. It's all fodder for our funny bone, and a great read for those days when you need a lift from your own fifty or sixty years of life."

~ Dr. Margaret Rutherford, Author, Clinical Psychologist, *drmargaretrutherford.com*

"Claflin's quirky wisdom is entertaining from start to finish!"

~ Marcia Kester Doyle, Author, *Who Stole My Spandex?*

"For all you macho men out there, don't worry. You don't need to be female to laugh along with, and sometimes even relate to, the hysterical stories shared in this book."

~ Michael J. Mele, *the-insane-asylum.blogspot.com*

"Vikki's book is better than Prozac."

~ Helene Cohen Bludman, *booksiswonderful.com*

"Mostly hilarious, but with poignancy, tenderness, and the finer things in life woven throughout, this book provides an intimate and beautiful look inside the world of someone who, quite frankly, I'd like to be when I grow up."

~ Lizzi Rogers, *summat2thinkon.wordpress.com*

"I plan on joining her Warrior Women Group to compete in the Best Boob Belt Award. I am confident I can at least be runner up. The group criteria includes: you must swear, be a grandma, and be in bed by 10 P.M. These are my peeps!"

~ Anne Bardsley, Author, *How I Earned My Wrinkles*

"A fast and fun read that delights in the everyday."

~ Lisa Carpenter, *grandmasbriefs.com*

"An honest, funny, and entertaining look at growing older, staying married, menopause, and motherhood in mid-life. A real treat for *all* moms."

~ Lisa Nolan, *monkeystarpressbooks.com*

ABOUT THE AUTHOR

Vikki Claflin is an award-winning humor writer and blogger, public speaker, and former newspaper columnist who lives in Hood River, Oregon. Her celebrated humor blog *Laugh Lines* shares the hilarious ups and down of midlife. She believes that laughter, a good glass of wine, and an econo-sized box of Milk Duds are the path to true Zen. Vikki has been featured on the *Michael J. Fox Foundation website*, *Erma Bombeck's Writer's Workshop*, *The Huffington Post*, *Scary Mommy*, *Better After 50*, and *Funny Times Magazine*. She also received a BlogHer14 "Voices of the Year" Humor award. Vikki's first book, *Shake, Rattle & Roll With It: Living & Laughing with Parkinson's*, was selected for Amazon.com's Editor's Favorite Books of 2014. It chronicles her hilarious and sometimes poignant journey living with Parkinson's disease.

Subscribe to her Blog at http://laugh-lines.net Laugh Lines
Friend her on Facebook here: https://facebook.com/laughlinesblog
Follow her on Twitter @vikkiclaflin

·

MORE GREAT READS FROM BOOKTROPE

Magic Fishing Panties by **Kimberly J. Dalferes** (Humor) A book that reminds all women of certain truths: the best pals are gal pals; all anyone needs to rule the world is a pair of black boots and a fabulous red coat; and above all else, live out loud, laugh often, and "occasionally" drink tequila.

The Girl's Guide to the Apocalypse by **Daphne Lamb** (Humor) Welcome to the Apocalypse. Your forecast includes acid rain, roving gangs and misplaced priorities, in this comedic take on the end of the world as we know it.

Three-Year-Olds Are A**holes by **Sarah Fader** (Humor) Three-year-old Samantha is determined to make a rainbow, no matter the cost to her mother's sanity. A story of love and frustration.

WASP Nest by **Lyn Eckfeldt** (Humorous) The first in a series of quirky mysteries, WASP Nest follows Lucy as she lands in Portland, Maine, to live with two roommates she met in recovery.

Who Stole My Spandex? Life in the Hot Flash Lane by **Marcia Kester Doyle** (Humor - Marriage & Family) A witty selection of stories from Doyle's madcap world of menopausal pitfalls, wardrobe malfunctions, and a family full of pranksters. No topic—no matter how crazy or unimaginable—is too taboo.

Would you like to read more books like these?
Subscribe to runawaygoodness.com, get a free ebook for signing up, and never pay full price for an ebook again.

Discover more books and learn about our
new approach to publishing at **booktrope.com**.

Made in the USA
Middletown, DE
26 April 2016